CISTERCIAN STUDIES SERIES: NUMBER ONE-HUNDRED AND FIVE

A SECOND LOOK AT
BERNARD OF CLAIRVAUX

CISTERCIAN STUDIES SERIES: NUMBER ONE-HUNDRED AND FIVE

A SECOND LOOK AT BERNARD OF CLAIRVAUX

by

Jean Leclercq

Translated by

Marie-Bernard Saïd

Cistercian Publications
Kalamazoo, Michigan
1990

A Translation of *Nouveau Visage de Bernard de Clairvaux. Approches psycho-historiques*. Paris: Les Editiones du Cerf, 1976.

The work of Cistercian Publications is made possible in part through support from Western Michigan University to The Institute of Cistercian Studies.

Cistercian Publications: Editorial Offices,
Institute of Cistercian Studies
Western Michigan University
Kalamazoo, MI 49008

Cistercian Publications are available in Britain and Europe
from Cassell Publishers
Artillery House, Artillery Row
London SW1P 1RT

Elsewhere, including Canada, orders should be sent to
Cistercian Publications Distribution:
Cistercian Publications
St Joseph's Abbey
Spencer, Massachusetts 01562

Library of Congress Cataloguing-in-Publication Data

Leclercq, Jean, 1911-
    [Nouveau visage de Bernard de Clairvaux. English]
    A second look at Bernard of Clairvaux / by Jean Leclercq:
    translated by Marie-Bernard Saïd.
       p. cm. --(Cistercian studies series; no.105)
    Translation of: Nouveau visage de Bernard de Clairvaux.
    ISBN 0-87907-605-4.--ISBN 0-87907-405-1 (pb.)
    1. Bernard, of Clairvaux,Saint,1090 or 91-1153--Psychology.
    I. Title. II. Series.
    BX4700.B5L3513 1989
    271'.12'024--dc19
    [B]   88-36544
                      CIP

Printed in the United States of America

TABLE OF CONTENTS

To Dom Augustine Moore
and to the
Monks of Conyers, Georgia
with gratitude

PREFACE TO THE ENGLISH EDITION

The main purpose of this Preface is to thank Father Pearse Aidan Cusack, of the Cistercian Abbey of Roscrea in Ireland, who improved the text of this little book after its first publication in French.

Twenty years after its publication, the pioneering study of Erik Erikson on *Young Man Luther* had been submitted to a thorough reexamination,[1] and the mere fact that it deserved such a treatment proves sufficiently that it was not insignificant. In a similar way, this attempt to apply the psycho-historical method to Bernard of Clairvaux is not expected to be more than a pioneering endeavor. The fact that various historians, including a President of the Bollandists,[2] have not condemned it is encouraging. When Fr Cusack did me the kindness of sharing his reservations with me and submitted to me the text of a planned review article,[3] I asked him to remedy some of the defects he had found in the book and he agreed to do so. May he find here the expression of my gratitude. In particular, he revised the chapter on irony, since my collaborator, Fr Robert Prentice OFM died before I could submit my redaction to him.

As Fr Cusack has shown in a doctrinal dissertation which one hopes will soon be published, there is no necessary incompatibility between the various 'modern psychologies'. All the same, the historian must, as I have asserted elsewhere, maintain his ability to be unbounded by the strict orthodoxy of any of them.[4] Human scientists sometimes appear less

1. *Psycho-history and Religion. The Case of the Young Man Luther*, edited by Roger A. Johnson (Philadelphia: Fortress Press, 1977).

2. B. de Gaiffier in *Analecta Bollandiana* 95 (1977) 445-446.

3. *Bernard of Clairvaux: A New Image (Book Review)*, in *Cistercian Studies* 39 (1977) 320-332.

4. *Monks and Love in the Twelfth Century France: Psycho-historical Essays* (Oxford University Press, 1978).

limited in their interpretations than historians, whose
hypotheses must remain founded upon facts and texts. In-
evitably, when they try to introduce a psychological approach into their methodology, an element of subjectivism is
to be expected. As one expert in this field has put it, 'We are
realizing increasingly that the psychoanalytic interpretation
reveals more about the psychoanalyst-reader than about the
author or his work...the real text is the subjective reaction of
the interpreter, influenced by his personal history, his individual subjectivity and his own way of understanding. Accordingly, what is obtained through analysis is, in fact,
merely the analyst's individual response to the stimulus of
the text'.[5]

Fr Cusack has produced a masterpiece of psycho-history in
interpreting a chapter of the legend of St Benedict according
to St Gregory,[6] and he is preparing a larger study on the
whole of the *Dialogues* along the same lines. Obviously, the
saints about whom we possess predominantly hagiographical
legends, such as St Anthony and St Benedict, have more significance as symbols than as historical individuals.[7] For
others, like St Bernard, in whose works we find much interesting autobiographical data, we are simultaneously faced
with the difficult task of interpretation. This cannot be done
satisfactorily the first time. This present series of essays follows upon other very different books on St Bernard. The
first of them, *Saint Bernard Mystique*, written in 1946,[8]
dealt mainly with what the saint taught about his own experience and his spiritual theology. Various volumes of studies
on the literary aspects of his writings prepared the way for a

5. A. Uleyn, 'A Psychological Approach to Mark's Gospel', in *Lumen
Vitae, International Review of Religious Education* 32 (1977) 480.

6. 'The Temptation of St Benedict: An Essay of Interpretation Through the
Literary Sources', in the *American Benedictine Review* 27 (1976) 143-163.

7. In an *Avant-propos* to B. de Gaiffier, *Recueil d' hagiographie* (Bruxelles,
1977) XI-XV, I have developed the idea more fully.

8. *St. Bernard mystique* (Bruges-Paris, 1948).

second general approach, which has appeared recently in English.[9] This new volume cannot claim to give a complete psychological portrait of St Bernard. Before this becomes possible, more short, detailed studies are needed. We must proceed by way of approximations before a definitive knowledge--to the extent that such a formula makes sense in history or in any other science--can be reached. Here is neither synthesis nor even last word on these topics. It is the hope of an old man that younger scholars will go further in this field and do better.

Last but far from least, I thank Sr Marie-Bernard Saïd OSB for her careful translation of this little work.

J L

Trinitytide 1978.

---

9. *Bernard of Clairvaux and the Cistercian Spirit* (Cistercian Publications, 1977). This volume summarizes articles collected in *Recueil d'études sur S. Bernard*, 3 vol. (Rome, 1962, 1966 and 1969); a fourth volume is being printed.

FOREWORD

PSYCHOLOGY AND THE SPIRITUAL LIFE

Almost thirty-five years ago, in 1953, at the eighth centenary of the death of Saint Bernard of Clairvaux, a voluminous and meritorious book was published containing much enlightening information on many aspects of his life and activities. The appendix to this book, *L'âme de Bernard. L'homme et le saint*,[1] in keeping with its title, deals simply with his soul, omitting any mention of temperament. Each paragraph of these final pages begins with the name of a virtue duly illustrated in the text. Not the slightest mention is made of faults, failings, or sins. Bernard stands out as eminently a saint. Yet, we cannot help wondering whether the 'real Bernard', the living man, was not left to one side. If this is true, and to the extent that it is, we are faced with a book which presents a Bernard who never existed.

Today, the progress of ecclesiology and christian historiography invites us to enquire how holiness, which comes from God, and sin, man's own doing, are reconciled in individual Christians and in the Church as a whole.[2] Yet, in dealing with those who have proved successful in one or another sphere, and especially in several spheres at once, it is not easy to be impartial. The majority of Bernard's contemporaries who wrote about him share their enthusiasm with us and this admiration has generally been passed on to succeeding centuries. Today, however, more than one historian tends to be severe with Bernard. Is it possible, we may ask, to pass fair judgement on him? In his writings we have the elements for a psychological analysis of the man's spiritual

1. *Bernard de Clairvaux* (Paris, 1953) 659-667.
2. Robert Kress, 'Ecclesiology and Mental Health', in *The American Ecclesiastical Review* 167 (1973) 91-101.

growth and it has been possible to extract a theory from his writings.[3] But, in actual practice, did Bernard really conform to this theory? Was he able to reconcile self-fulfillment and union with God. And if so, how?

These questions cannot be answered in generalities. What we need is some sort of clinical judgement. But is this possible? Such is the aim of psycho-history. Although applying this discipline to persons of medieval times presents a number of difficulties, it also offers possibilities, as I have shown in various essays published elsewhere.[4]

Applying psychological methods to Bernard of Clairvaux can reveal in him more or less conscious mechanisms and motivations which he did not always express and then lead us to assess the facts in the light of the christian values he declared he served.

Is it possible for us to know to what extent he integrated his psychism and his intentions? There is no doubt that these both existed in the man Bernard and we should not shirk considering honestly both the one and the other. There is in him the saint, but there is also, and primarily, the man who must be examined as objectively as possible. At the outset of a long series of psycho-historical studies of several of his texts one of the members of the research team confessed to having set out with a prior bias in favor of Bernard simply because he was a saint. It was necessary to point out that history is, so to speak, a profane science when it comes to such preconceived ideas.

The field open to investigation is very vast. It is impossible to examine here all of Bernard's behaviors in the light of

3. Robert P. Stepsis, 'Fulfillment of Self and Union with God in the Writings of Bernard of Clairvaux', in *The American Benedictine Review* 24 (1973) 348-364.

4. Already appeared are: 'Modern Psychology and the Interpretation of Medieval Texts', in *Speculum. A Journal of Medieval Studies* 48 (1973) 476-490; 'Psycho-history and the Understanding of Medieval People', in *The Hanoverian* 6 (1975) 6-9 and 7 (1975) 7-10.

his texts. We must necessarily limit ourselves in these preliminary approaches to typifying only a few of them. I have
had the good fortune of studying them in collaboration with
a psychoanalyst, a psycholinguist, a group of psychologists,
and a doctor. Furthermore, several members of the team
were also medievalists. I am grateful to them for their help
but shoulder entirely any responsibility for shortcomings
there may be in the presentation of the results, which in no
way pretend to be either complete or definitive.

The order in which the different essays of this book have
been arranged is necessarily artificial because each text, or
group of texts, has been studied separately, sometimes with
different collaborators, uninfluenced by my other collaborators, a fact which guarantees greater objectivity. The
grouping of the texts aims at leading the reader from historical and literary aspects to spiritual issues. Yet, it will be
noticed, everything tends to intertwine, just as it did in Saint
Bernard, the man, under observation, and if there is some
repetition it is doubtless revealing of certain dominant elements in his character.

I would like to express my thanks here to all those who
have helped me in the preparation of this little book as well
as those who assured me congenial conditions for writing it,
in particular the abbot and monks of Holy Spirit Abbey,
Conyers, Georgia.

JL

In the following pages, titles not preceded by the name of an
author are publications where I have had an opportunity to
deal more specifically with subjects which can only be al-
luded to here.

Chapter I

BERNARD'S FIRST BIOGRAPHER

I. THE PROBLEMS RAISED BY THE VITA PRIMA

It is our good fortune to have a very beautiful account of the life of Saint Bernard begun during his lifetime and continued shortly after his death by contemporaries who had known him.[1] Here then is a source of information which would seem to be trustworthy and one which all his biographers have drawn.[2]   But was this not a proof of naive credulity? The genesis of this text has been studied with a very mature critical mind by A. H. Bredero,[3] who is now skeptical about the value of this document; it cannot fail to lead historical research, including that conducted according to a psychological method, down a blind alley.[4] And indeed, not only does it have recourse to the artificial processes of the hagiographical genre, often very little trustworthy, not only was it begun without Bernard's knowledge,[5] consequently without the possibility of consulting the man who knew his own past best, but even more, the text underwent successive revisions designed to facilitate Bernard's canonization, and they had the result of modifying the image

---

1. The text is in PL 185:225-368.

2. I did this in *S. Bernard mystique* (Bruges-Paris, 1948).

3. *Études sur la 'Vita prima' de S. Bernard* (Rome, 1960); this volume of 184 pages brings together three articles which appeared in *Analecta* 17 (1961) 3-72, 215-260, and 18 (1962) 3-59.

4. A.H. Bredero, 'The Canonization of St. Bernard and the Rewriting of his Life', in J.R. Sommerfeldt, ed., *Cistercian Ideals and Reality*, Cistercian Studies Series 60 (Kalamazoo, 1978) 80-105.

5. William of Saint Thierry, *Vita Prima* 1, *Praefatio*; PL 185:226C.

which the authors of the account wanted to present.[6]

Other documents of the same genre have, however, offered matter for scientific researches which are not without some interest, conducted by historians or psycho-historians like Richter,[7] Nitschke,[8] Goodich,[9] and, in the case of Peter Damian, Lester K. Little, who has restored new value to the account of this saint's life by John of Lodi, and its right to be used for objective history, something which many,[10] including myself,[11] had denied.[12]

The *First Life of Saint Bernard* is made up of five books, the first of which was written by William of Saint Thierry, who says he had long conversations with Saint Bernard and, certainly, had known him personally.[13] After William's death in 1148—five years before Bernard's death—the work was continued by a benedictine abbot, who composed a second book, and who had been designated for this task, less because he had seen Bernard frequently than because he was acknowledged to be a gifted writer.[14] Books three to five

6. Bredero, 'The Canonization', 80-105.

7. H. Richter, *Die Personlichkeitsdarstellungen in cluniazensischen Absviten*. Inaugural speech at the University of Erlangen-Nürnberg (1972) offset.

8. A. Nitschke, *Heilige in dieser Welt* (Stuttgart, 1962).

9. M. Goodich, 'Childhood and Adolescence Among the Thirteenth-Century Saints', in *History of Childhood Quarterly* 1 (1973) 285-309.

10. André Wilmart, 'Une lettre de S. Pierre Damien a l'impératrice Agnés', in *Revue Bénédictine* 44 (1972).

11. Jean Leclercq, *S. Pierre Damien ermite et homme d'Église* (Rome, 1960) 17-19.

12. Lester K. Little, 'The Personal Development of Peter Damian', in *Order and Innovation. Essays in Honor of Joseph R. Strayer*, edd. W.C. Jordan, B. McNals, T.F. Rinz (1976).

13. A first meeting took place towards the end of 1119 or before the autumn 1120, according to Stanislaus Ceglar, *William of St. Thierry, The Chronology of his Life...*, Diss. Catholic University of America (Washington, D.C., 1971) 414. On William as the author of Book One, see Bredero, *Études*, pp. 100-109.

14. Bredero, *Ibid.*, pp. 109-116.

were composed by Geoffrey of Auxerre, who had been a close collaborator of Bernard from 1140 onward and whose witness, therefore, undoubtedly deserves our attention.[15] Thus, a priori, there is nothing to exclude this text being used for a life history.[16]

But how shall we proceed? We must be wary of a method which consists in projecting undiscerningly identical literary or psychological schemata on various persons, especially when they belonged to cultures which are more or less foreign to those in which and for which these processes of psychological analysis have been developed. But at least we may confront the facts presented by hagiography with those known from other sources, whether they are contemporary witnesses or the writings of the person in question. With Saint Bernard, we seem to be favored by the fact that he has left us treatises, sermons, and especially some five hundred or so letters; and even though these last are more public documents than 'confidential letters', they hold immense interest and their study is never disappointing.

But, the method must be rigorous. We must clearly distinguish what the text teaches us, on the one hand, about the subject of the narrative—Saint Bernard—and on the other, the author, in the present case, the authors, of the account. For it can happen that a *Life* tells us more about the author than the subject.[17] The *First Life* gives us three images of Saint Bernard, we might almost be tempted to say 'three different Bernards': William's, Ernold's, and Geoffrey's. Do they agree? Can they be, as it were, super-imposed? Just as the texts of the New Testament let us know the Jesus of Mat-

---

15. *Ibid.*, pp. 116-138.

16. The expression is of Bruce Mazlisch, 'What is Psycho-History?' in *The Transactions of the Royal Historical Society,* Fifth Series, 21 (London 1971) 79-99.

17. This is what has been shown in connection with Stephen of Obazine, under the title 'Modern Psychology and the Interpretation of Medieval Texts', in *Speculum* 48 (1973) 476-490.

thew, Mark, Luke, John, and Paul, or the texts about Saint Francis of Assisi give us the successive ideas people had of him, so with Bernard, only a comparison with other documents will allow us to verify the historical nature of the account. And if we are led to reduce, or even to deny, the historicity of what is narrated, we shall at least, to some extent, know something about the teller, and this in itself, is worthwhile.

We cannot here exhaust such a broad and delicate subject for its study would require the meeting and conferring of specialists in hagiography, psycho-history, and psycholinguistics, a pooling and confrontation of their findings and research which would have to be conducted independently of one another. In the present state of works we shall have to be content with simply stating the problems and suggesting a few pointers to their solution. These will have to do with themes or schemata which obviously stand out at a first reading of the *First Life* and, in this, just Book One, written by William of Saint Thierry.

II. PROBLEMS RAISED BY BOOK ONE

Book One itself does not fail to raise a particular problem. We would be inclined to think that William is going to give a series of first-hand information about the childhood, youth and monastic beginnings of Bernard. He had talked with him more than once and had had the opportunity of asking him about his past, even if we suppose that Bernard did not volunteer this information. During his visits to Clairvaux, William had been able to talk with Gerard and Bernard's other brothers, and to ask them questions. Even, elsewhere in the foundations, these same and other relatives or companions of Bernard surely told what they knew about the life of the man of God to whom they had been so close. Judging by the way in which we today think of a biography, we would expect these precise and sure memories to have found their way into William's account.

What was the real situation? By his own admission, William's purpose was not to write down the facts which had marked Bernard's life: he intended leaving this to others who would tell of his life and death, later on. His intention was to make known not what, in Bernard, is mysterious, 'impenetrable, inexpressible, that is to say the presence of Christ acting and speaking in him, but his actions to the extent that they reveal something of the invisible purity of his inner holiness and of his conscience'.[18] Thus, from among the facts he knew, William made a selection. For example, he does not say a word about the *Apologia* which he urged Bernard to write, nor does he mention the keen controversy to which it was linked. And on matters on which he decided to speak, he goes about what has been called 'conscious legend-making'.[19] Instead of calling upon his personal memories, he founded his account on the *Fragments* written down by Geoffrey of Auxerre, and he used them according to the laws of hagiography, whose aim is not only to instruct, nor even to 'interest', but to 'edify'.[20] But as William was always an author and a thinker of some originality, he tried to cover up the fact that he was adopting the conventional model. Yet, if we compare his work to earlier or contemporary *Lives*, and even with the other books of this *First Life*, we can recognize many a traditional theme in what he says about the way Bernard prayed, became absorbed in meditation, refrained from eating and sleeping, or about his brothers' opposition to his healing activities, the way he re-

18. *Vita prima 1, Praefatio*; PL 185:226B-227A.

19. The expression 'légendarisation consciente' is from Bredero, *Études, p. 109.*

20. *These expressions are from H. Delehaye, Les légendes hagiographiques 2* (Brussels, 1906) 77. On medieval monastic hagiography, see evidence in *The Love of Learning and the Desire for God*[3] (New York, 1982) 164-168.

ceived his as-yet-worldly sister Humbeline and brought about her conversion.[21] All this is part of the intentional legend-making which was, very early on, practiced in cistercian circles, in connection with the origins and the expansion of the Order,[22] and to which Bernard himself had probably contributed, in the measure to which he influenced the redaction of texts relative to the origins.[23] William contributed to this 'tendentious presentation' of the facts in writing about Bernard; he aimed at highlighting the part he played in spreading his Order.[24]

Thus, the *First Life* is already an interpretation of what Bernard had been, to the point of making it 'almost impossible to submit all of William's information to a critical examination and to isolate the basic reality; his account almost entirely eludes such discernment'.[25] He 'stresses even more the miraculous contained in Geoffrey's information',[26] and he did so in his own way, adding his own sauce. For example, he gives much greater importance to Bernard's mother, whereas, in the *Fragments* Geoffrey had given first place to his father. This too depended on William's general intention: if he stresses the holiness of the mother, it was because in his opinion, Bernard was withdrawn from the world already at birth, and by his extraordinary holiness—a theme current in hagiography of the day.[27] Likewise, a conversation which, according to Geoffrey's text, was an ordinary everyday discussion between Bernard and his brother Gerard, about the economical difficulties of the monastery, becomes a long complaint of Gerard which covers over a

---

21. Bredero, *Études*, p. 104 and p. 130, n.3, has given other examples and references.

22. *Ibid.*, pp. 59 and 72.

23. Cp. *Recueil d'études sur S. Bernard* 2 (Rome, 1969) 180.

24. Bredero, *Études*, p. 104.

25. *Ibid.*

26. *Ibid.*, p. 105.

27. *Ibid.*

reproach aimed at Bernard.[28] Other facts are passed over in silence or interpreted in keeping with another of William's intentions, which was to defend Bernard against criticisms of his interventions in religious politics, and consequently to integrate into the recognized norms of holiness certain dubious facts of his conduct and character.[29] This led William to stress the ambiguity in Bernard and to show some of the problematic sides of his personality. This necessity allowed William to come to a deep understanding of the personality he was writing about.[30] Yet, he could not avoid understanding Bernard according to his own standards, which we shall have to discern later on.

At least we can already grasp both the limits and the value of Book One: limits, because William made his selection in view of aims which have nothing to do with historical objectivity; interest and importance, because 'the image William creates of Bernard's life and holiness determined that of those who carried on his work, even though they did not come up to his expectations'.[31] It is legitimate for us then to study first the part of the First Life which he wrote. Not everything there is invented; it is in no way a fairy story. But the question is to know whether this work is primarily a historical source, or a doctrinal and psychological witness.

III. SOME THEMES AND THEIR MEANING

There is no need to dwell on themes which are obviously hagiographical commonplaces. In the passage that says that Bernard was so recollected, so interior, that he never noticed whether the church of his monastery was vaulted or not, we

28. *Ibid.*, p. 106.
29. *Ibid.*, p. 108.
30. *Ibid.*, p. 109.
31. *Ibid.*, p. 103.

immediately recognize something which had often been written about saints in the past.[32] In fact, this idea does not at all coincide with what we otherwise know about Bernard's very keen sense of observation. What is said about the way he refused to receive his sister, then only agreed to do so on the condition that she renounce the world, is similar to accounts which were read in the Lives of the Desert Fathers.[33] Again, the theme of the texts to which Bernard's chastity was submitted recalls many other texts of the same kind.[34] Again, it is not uninteresting to suppose that William chose it and used it in order to answer to something which worried either Bernard, or himself, or his readers. We shall probably never know which of these three conjectures corresponds to reality. For if William did not say everything he knew about Bernard, the fact that he decided to say what he did reveals the way he interpreted what he knew.

A theme which comes up in the opening lines of the narrative seems to betray one of the author's orientations. He recalled the ancient fervor of the primitive Church and early monasticism.[35] This theme is found further on in the story,[36]

32. Vita prima 1.20; PL 185:238.

33. An example taken from the Apoththegmata (Helladius 1) [PG 65:173A; The Sayings of the Desert Fathers, Cistercian Studies 59 (1984) 62] is quoted and situated in the tradition by A. Guillaumont, 'Le dépaysement comme forme d'ascése dans le monachisme ancien', in Annuaire de l'École Pratique des Hautes-Études, Section des sciences religieuses 76 (1968-1969) 55. Other accounts parallel to that of the conversion of Humbeline are quoted by Philip Rousseau, 'Blood-Relationships among Early Eastern Ascetics', in The Journal of Theological Studies 23 (1972) 136, and by Louis Leloir, 'Solitude and sollicitude. Le moine loin et prés du monde, d'aprés les "Paterica" arméniens', in Irénikon 47 (1973) 312-313 and 319.

34. 'Agressivité et répression chez Bernard de Clairvaux', in Revue d'histoire de la spiritualité (1976) 47-64. The fact has been pointed out by a specialist in medieval hagiography: G. Philippart, 'Vitae patrum. Trois travaux récents sur d'anciennes traductions latines', in Analecta Bollandiana 92 (1974) 365.

35. Vita prima, Praef.; PL 185:225.

36. Ibid., 15, 235 and 34; 247.

and in the form it should normally have in the life of an abbot. Hagiographers were fond of paying attention to the Church of apostolic times, and then the Church of the age of the martyrs. The beginnings of monasticism were substituted for this latter period, a utopian model, so to speak. Manifestly, William took advantage of the examples given by Bernard, or which he attributed to him, in order to propose his own program of monastic reform and to hold up Bernard as the ideal image of the abbot and his community at Clairvaux as a model abbey. As Bernard had given a theological interpretation of cistercian phenomenon,[37] William elaborated the theology of the life lived at Clairvaux in the days of Saint Bernard, and in doing so he elaborated a theology of the cistercian phenomenon as a whole.[38] Once more we are faced with a 'committed' historiography, designed to illustrate ideas more than relate facts. In this perspective,the reformed man, the man in whom we see the achievement of the reforming program which must be applied to the whole Church, the man who is, in this sense, a success, is the saint.[39]

IV. THE MOTHER IMAGE AND FAMILY BACKGROUND

Very early on, in this account, also appears the important part played in Bernard's life by his family background and, in particular, the part played by his mother in his vocation to the monastic life. Certainly, this last idea was very frequent in hagiography. Numerous examples of premonitory dreams, some of which are exactly like the one William attributes to Bernard's mother when she was carrying him, have been

37. 'Les intentions des fondateurs de l'Ordre cistercian', *Collectanea Cisterciensia* 30 (1968) 245-258.

38. *Vita prima* 35; 247-248.

39. 'L'historiographie monastique de Léon IX à Callixte II', in *Il monachesimo e la riforma ecclesiastica (1049-1122)*, (Milan, 1971) 271-301.

collected and studied.[40] Likewise, the fact that the mother image influences, sometimes decisively, the appearance of a vocation to monastic life, has been observed in western christian culture of the thirteenth century[41] and our own day.[42] Perhaps it is a transcultural fact. There is nothing surprising at finding it in the *First Life*. And yet it recurs with exceptional frequency, insistence, and precision. Almost all that M. Goodich writes about the childhood of thirteenth-century saints is to be found in Saint Bernard's youth too.[43] But what is often mere general allusion, in the sources he has examined—confirmed, however, by what we know of family life at that period— is personalized and interiorized when William writes of Bernard.

At the start, he stated that Aleth, Bernard's mother, loved her son so much that she did not put him into the care of a wet-nurse.[44] Then William tells about the dream she had during her pregnancy.[45] There seems to be more here than the commonplace of the portent of a great future: it foretells the influence the mother was to have on her son. Indeed, we perceive at once an astonishingly precise formula, one which delights contemporary psychologists when they hear it

40. Numerous witnesses have seen assembled by F. Lanzoni, 'Il sogno presagio della madre incinta nella letteratura medievale e antica', in *Analecta Bollandiana* 45 (1927) 225-261.

41. M. Goodich, 'Childhood and Adolescence', (n.9) pp. 285-287. Examples of 'maternal influence' in the Middle Ages have also been cited by Mary M. McLaughlin, in Lloyd de Mause, *History of Childhood* (New York, 1974) 91, 115-116, 124-127, 135, 167.

42. A. Riva, *Sulla psicodinamica della vocazione religiosa* (Milan, 1979) 31-37: 'Relazioni con la madre'; K.G. Rey, *Das Mutterbild des Priesters. Zur psychologie des Priesteberufes* (Zürich, 1969); J. Bariavic, *Les images parentales dans la psychologie du séminariste et du prêtre*, typed thesis, Brussels (Lumen vitae) 1971-1972, pp. 123-127 and *passim*. Cp. also A. Manaranche, *L'Esprit et la femme* (Paris, 1974) 152 .

43. 'Childhood', p. 289: brothers and sisters accompanying one of their family in the religious life is cited.

44. *Vita prima* 1.1; PL 185:227C.

45. *Ibid.*, 3;228.

quoted: 'He realized his mother's desire'.[46] Fidelity to the memory of Aleth's desire was to be essential when the time came for Bernard to decide on his future, a decision which led him to enter Cîteaux.[47] He used this same argument to 'convert' his brothers and his sister to monastic life.[48] And the idea recurs again further on.[49]

These are the texts. What do they mean? The significance of what they say appears extremely important for the psychoanalyst: one of the most characteristic alienations is to realize the mother's desire for the person and it is the contrary attitude to which the patient must be restored. This maternal desire was symbolized by the dream Aleth had before Bernard's birth, and it was this desire, fulfilled by Aleth herself during her saintly life, that Bernard imposed on his sister.[50] Even in hagiographical literature, such emphasis on this theme is rare. But, we may ask, does it correspond to reality with Bernard, or to a 'Bernard fantasy' conjured up by William? How can we find out for sure?

There exists, it is true, a still unedited letter attributed to Bernard, which is supposed to have been written to Aleth after she had become a nun.[51] But this document is apocryphal: Aleth died in 1103 or 1104, when Bernard was fourteen or fifteen years old.[52] Her husband, Tescelin became

---

46. *Ibid.*, 3;228.

47. *Ibid.*, 9;231.

48. *Ibid.*, 10;232.

49. Ceglar, pp. 11-12, has pointed out that Aleth is presented by William of Saint Thierry as a model christian wife; he adds that it is possible that William had also thought of his own mother when he described Aleth: 'She seemed to be an example of the good influence a mother can have on her milieu, just as the case of Humbeline illustrates the triumph of grace over the attractions of the world'.

50. *Vita prima* 1.30;245.

51. 'Nouveaux témoins de la survie de S. Bernard', *Homenaje a Fray Justo Pérez de Urbel* (Silos, 1977) 93-109.

52. Cp. *Bernard de Clairvaux* (Paris, 1953) p. 26, n.63.

became a monk.[53] The claim that she became a nun is legendary. Yet it does not lack significance to the extent that people thought she had, or could have, one day realized her desire, otherwise than in her son Bernard, and fulfilled her own wish, something we can express by modifying slightly William's words: 'His mother realized her desire'. Evidence of a monk writing to his mother or, more frequently, about his mother after her death, is provided elsewhere.[54] Still, it would be embarrassing to think that Bernard could have sent Aleth the exhortations, even the reprimands, we find in this text. For many reasons, then, it provides no light for us.

The means of verifying whether this mother-image corresponds to reality in William or in Bernard remains, then, those which have already been indicated: the juxtaposition of these texts with all the other sources we have on both men, then the juxtaposition of their own writings with evidence from their contemporaries. Already we see that if the mother image was as important for Bernard as William claimed, many features of his character and work would be explained. For example, reading Letter Two which Bernard wrote to Fulk, a young canon regular, with its strong abuse of the young man's uncle, a psychologist knowing nothing about Bernard's life would immediately, as soon as he noticed certain structures in the text, ask whether Bernard had been strongly attached to his mother or not.[55] Likewise the affection Bernard said he had for his brother Gerard, and his sorrow at his death, lead us to wonder whether he had

53. According to the necrology of Saint-Bénigne, cited in PL 185:243, n.63, Tescelin had 'withdrawn' to Clairvaux, according to *Bernard de Clairvaux*, p. 37, n.66.

54. We may, for example, think of the long twelfth-century epitaph in letter form sent by Peter the Venerable to his kinsfolk after the death of his mother Raingarde. She, probably like Bernard's mother, 'desired' to become a nun. The text is in Giles Constable, *The Letters of Peter the Venerable* (Cambridge, Mass., 1967) 1:153-173; on Peter the Venerable and his mother, see the reference in volume 2, p. 420.

55. See below, Chapter III.

not found in Gerard the means of compensating for a mother's love he missed.[56] His deep devotion to the Blessed Virgin would also be worth studying from this point of view.[57] And in several conflicts, Bernard's conduct could be partly explained according to the same viewpoint.

What William lets us see is a relationship, not only with his mother, but with a whole family tissue which acted on him and which he himself influenced. Already the fact that he succeeded in bringing to Cîteaux all his brothers, including the eldest, would be enough to reveal a very strong, even domineering, personality in him; for if this ascendancy of a younger over an elder brother surprises us in the modern western culture, how much more surprising it is when we recall the family structure of the twelfth century. From a psychological point of view, family relationships are "piégées", as we say today, and William saw that already he tells of conflicts Bernard had with his brothers, and his uncle, and says they sometimes reproached him actively.[58]

We see it is even in the accounts of 'miracles' which have nothing very original about them but in which William tried to bring us this theme. Did he do so in order somehow to create a crisis, intended to show that Bernard, patient in face of reproaches, was a saint? In at least one letter Bernard confesses that he once flew into a violent rage against one of his brothers, Barthelemy.[59] Did that never happen in other circumstances which he never happened to mention in writing? Is the 'motherly

56. SC 26. 3-14; SBOp 1 (Rome, 1957) 171-181.

57. At least this is what some of Bernard's biographers think when they uncritically believe everything William wrote on this mother theme, which reflects more William's psychology. Moreover, we know that Bernard's devotion to Mary was ardent but far from as original as has for long been thought on the basis of writings which are not his.

58. *Vita prima* 1.43-45; PL 185; 252-253.

59. Ep 70; SBOp 7 (Rome, 1974) 173. This incident is discussed under the title 'Saint Bernard et la communauté', *Collectanea cisterciensia* 34 (1972) 77-79; in M.B. Pennington ed., *Contemplative Community*, CS 21 (1972) 61-113.

love' which William attributed to Bernard with his brothers[60] merely William's projection? It is moreover combined with another, more surprising fantasy which makes Bernard out to be fatherly towards his brothers.[61] Certainly both these ideas—to be a mother or a father—are themes we find elsewhere, and they have sometimes been attributed to saints after their deaths, although they had themselves refused such images.[62] But the fact that William chose these themes in preference to others, reveals something of himself, and perhaps something in Bernard. It would be instructive then to discern what the authors of the other books of the *First Life* selected and kept, and to verify whether that coincides with what William says.

While waiting for the detailed study that William's psychology deserves, we may already remark that, according to the *Old Life* written about him on the basis of memories kept alive in one of the places he had lived, he had at least two visions of the Virgin Mary. In at least two cases, she is

60. *Vita prima* 1.43; PL 185;242.

61. *Ibid.*, 27;242. Just as in the days of the Desert Fathers Poemen's brothers 'accepted him as more than a brother: they went to him as to a spiritual father': see Rousseau, (n.33) pp. 141-151. The author concludes, p. 144, with remarks which could be applied to the origins of Clairvaux: 'A close union between members of a same family seems to have existed specially at the beginning of ascetic careers, or during times of crisis and dissolution. There is no doubt that a greater familiarity with one another, habits of dependence, the acceptance of seniority due to age, forced men placed in such situations to affront the tensions inherent to common life in ways that they would not otherwise have known. Such pressures had more importance in the case of men like Poemen and Pachomius who held key positions in the development of the monastic movement'. Nearer our day, we think of the importance of her family for Saint Thérèse of Lisieux, before her entry into Carmel, and afterwards. For Saint Bernard's age another case where the 'whole family entered religion' in the story of the deacon Nicholas, who became a Premonstratensian, is told by F. Petit, *La spiritualité des prémontrés aux XIIᵉ et XIIIᵉ siècles* (Paris, 1947) 70-71. The author writes, not without some exaggeration: 'The conversations of whole families giving themselves to religion in order to lead the apostolic life abroad in the twelfth century.'

62. J.F. Gilmont, 'Paternité et médiation du fondateur d'Ordre', in *Revue d'ascétique et de mystique* 40 (1964) 393-426.

said to have taken a very 'motherly' attitude towards him first by taking him to her heart in order to console him, and then, when he was ill, by bringing him furs which were more comfortable than the coarse cloth with which he was covered.[63] Do we not have here a curious coincidence between themes applied to William and those he applied to Bernard?

V. A SPIRITUAL JOURNEY ACCORDING TO WILLIAM OR IS IT BERNARD?

One of the events in William's Book One on Bernard has interested biographers most—because it is rare in this sort of text. It describes a long, painful inner crisis which led the young abbot of Clairvaux from uncompromising strictness to moderation. First, he fell ill through excessive austerity. Then he was overcome by sadness,[64] 'distress';[65] strangely enough, it was a non-monk—who was, however, a canon regular—William of Champeaux, bishop of Châlons, who came to teach this monk, this abbot, who was later to become a theologian of the christian and monastic life, the correct spirituality.[66] William insists a great deal on this slow maturation, this educational process, which little by little led Bernard to a correct appreciation of man and his attitude to God, and let him discover that all pleasure is not evil.[67] This runs all through the account and it certainly corresponds to one of William's intentions.

63. 'Pour un portrait de Guillaume de Saint Thierry', *Saint Thierry une abbaye du VIᵉ au XXᵉ siècle* (Saint Thierry, 1979) 413-28; ET 'Towards a Spiritual Portrait of William of Saint Thierry', *William Abbot of St Thierry*, CS 94 (Kalamazoo, 1987) 204-224.

64. *Vita prima* 1.22-24; PL 185:239-242.

65. *Ibid.*, 26;242.

66. *Ibid.*, 32;246.

67. *Ibid.*, 40-41;250-251.

Does it also correspond to something Bernard experienced? Do the words William attributed to Bernard on
the motivation for the monastic vocation—to die entirely to
the world[68]—not express his own idea? Is the discourse he
puts into Bernard's mouth about the need everyone has, who
wants to enter Clairvaux, to leave his body at the door and to
live solely by the spirit,[69] in keeping with Bernard's
anthropology or William's? Only a comparison with the
teachings of each would let us see if they verify this and
other assertions of the same kind. On the basis of Bernard's
works, it is difficult to discern in him an evolution on the
important points concerning man and his relationship with
God. But had this evolution occurred before he started writing? There certainly seems to be a certain intolerance in his
texts and in his behavior; but we can also pick out many
signs of his 'humanity', indulgence, moderation;[70] and the
impression he left to those who had lived close to him was
one of a pleasant, joyful man.[71]

Within this anthropological problem it does indeed seem
that there lies another and deeper one which is perhaps
unique to the thinker-philosopher-theologian that William
was. He insists a great deal on the difficulty of the use of
words in Bernard and about him: 'I do not think we can describe the marvels of his life, or the way he led an angelic
life on earth, unless we live by the same spirit he did....[72]
When he spoke of the realities of the spiritual life and the
edification of souls, he spoke to men in the tongue of angels,
and he was scarcely understood.... They could not grasp

68. *Ibid.*, 20;238.
69. *Ibid.*
70. In evidence see the texts presented as 'letters of humanity' in *S.
Bernard. Lettres choisies* (Namur, 1962).
71. Cp. 'S. Bernard parmi nous. Dix années d'études bernardines', in
Collectanea Cisterciensia 36 (1974) 20-21.
72. *Vita prima* 1.19; PL 185:237.

what he was saying....[73] In his preaching, the monks reverenced what they did not understand....[74] He accused himself of ignorance and deplored the necessity of having to break silence when he did not know how to speak....[75]

William seems to have taken some pleasure in analyzing Bernard's long crisis of word and intelligence, which was ended only by the intervention of 'a strong-worded man',[76] William of Champeaux. Already before that, in connection with a miracle by which Bernard got his brother Gerard out of prison, William had remarked that Gerard's eyes 'were restrained from seeing and he did not know what happened to him'.[77] Later on, Josbert of Ferté, whom Bernard was to heal, had 'lost his intelligence and speech'.[78]

How much in all this is objectively historical? Part of these states of soul had come about before Bernard and William met; what did the latter really know about them? Did Bernard later confide in him? Or is it merely phantasmagoria, an image William had of Bernard, what he had seen in him, perhaps without Bernard's knowledge? This would not rule out a basis on something true: sometimes, others see in us aspects of ourselves which we refuse to acknowledge or to accept because they are too true. But, do the texts Bernard has left us show him hesitating, doubting of himself, knowing periods of physical weariness, psychic depression, distress about the message he had to deliver, no longer speaking, withdrawing into solitude because he cannot find the words, does not know what to say? Before having gone into a psycholinguistic analysis of all his works, we cannot yet say. The body of his work is vast, varied, and subtle, revealing a complex and refined character. Like

73. *Ibid.*, 28;243.
74. *Ibid.*, 29;243.
75. *Ibid.*, 243;244.
76. *Ibid.*, 37;249.
77. *Ibid.*, 12;234.
78. *Ibid.*, 43;252.

every other man, he must have known such moments. We see the admission of this, for example, in the rhetoric of his letter to Eskil of Lund, a late letter, it is true, written a year before his death. There he says 'I'm tired out'.[79] But the general impression we have so far of what he says and does is more that of an energetic man, quite sure of himself—many people would be inclined to say too sure. We are brought round, then, to thinking that what William was describing here was a crisis of knowledge and word going on in himself and ascribed to Bernard.

This impression seems confirmed by the *Old Life* of William. Much is said there about William's 'labors', 'temptations', 'hesitations'. Even after his death he is presented as waiting an entire year before giving a posthumous answer he had promised, and when he did give it, it consisted partly in imposing a fresh, delay. As much as he took pleasure in thinking and writing, he was powerless to speak, unable to take action in the very difficult circumstances in which the situation of his abbey of Saint Thierry placed him. He left in order to avoid these concerns. He seems to have been sickly, undecided, depressive, all natural weaknesses which brought suffering on him, but also provided great spiritual enrichment, a deep and refined religious experience.

VI. BERNARD, A MYSTERY ELUDING HISTORY

How can we end these provisional clues other than by outlining a methodology and stating its limits? The conditions for verifying the historical objectivity of the *First Life* would require the juxtaposition of the various books with the writings of their authors; for William of Saint Thierry, Ernold of Bonneval, and Geoffrey of Auxerre have all left behind, sometimes abundant, literature, some of it, in Geoffrey's

79. Ep 390.2; SBOp 8 (Rome, 1977).

case still unedited. Then it would be necessary to compare them with one another, and finally with the writings of Saint Bernard. In the course of this immense work the use of computers would reveal constants and differences in vocabulary and means of expression, and thus of thought. There would then remain a comparison of the successive states of the various books of the *First Life*. By this we would discover something of each author's intentions, then those of the revisors. It would then be necessary to examine anything significant for psychology, including certain aporias, such as the allusion William makes to the 'bandits' cave'[80] which may correspond to reality, but may also have some symbolic meaning, unless it is simply a biblical reminiscence; perhaps this last possibility does not exclude the previous two. Anyone can see that so vast a project remains to be carried out as to be discouraging.

Perhaps William himself points us to a different, apparently negative answer, one that would reconcile the requirements and the limitations of both history and psychology. Because, all things considered, is it not utopic, or illusory, to want to discover an 'historical' Bernard? Jesus spoke about himself and his message in parables. Francis of Assisi spoke enigmatically. William of Saint Thierry, a man of intense interior life did not worry over the relationship between understanding and words, without some reason, as if he wanted to bring his reader round to asking, as he did, questions incapable of clear answers. Was he not trying to suggest at once his own mystery and Bernard's and to set his own before the reader using Bernard's merely as a pretext? On this level objective historicity no longer counts. When he presents Bernard 'doubting his own zeal',[81] does he pretend

---

80. *Vita prima* 1.25; PL 185:241: *spelunca latronum*, a biblical expression (Jer 7:11; Mk 11:17; Lk 19:46); further on in the *Vita prima* 35 (248A), an allusion to the cavern (*spelunca*) seems to refer to the one where Saint Benedict lived at Subiaco.

81. *Vita prima* 1.29; PL 185;243.

to say what was really going on in Bernard? Was he not reconstructing him more according to what he himself experienced? Was he not giving an illustration of his own knowledge of man? Was he not putting theory into images? Could Book One of the *First Life* be, so to speak, the cartoon of his own anthropology? But this is realized in Bernard as in himself, and in us and in this sense, what William lets us see in this book describes Bernard yet does not describe him, betrays and yet does not betray him. In some way it is an exercise in applied anthropology, and the actual events were, for William, of only secondary importance.

A certain reassuring scholarship would like to find answers to all these questions; but in presence of the mystery of man and his encounter with God, the spiritual teacher William of Saint Thierry felt disconcerted. It was enough for him to have approached the mystery of man, every man, by projecting on to it a little of the light he had in himself and of the images which reflected it. He did not pretend to explain everything: he chose certain themes, like maternal influence, either because he had heard Bernard speak of it, or because he had an intuition of it some other way, or, again, because he had had a similar experience himself. In any case, he decided to dwell on this theme and to make it one of the keys of his whole story. To discern what he retained and what he left out among the facts at his disposal would provide a difficult path for interpreting this, and bringing to light what William thought of Bernard: the key-word is perhaps the one never used; what William never dared say about Bernard is perhaps most important for letting us know the naked truth about him. We shall probably never know— at least by the text—what William was hiding from us, or, consequently, who Bernard really was. In reading the text we are impressed by the aporias, by a sort of unknowing: to the degree that he makes us ask questions, the abyss deepens before him, before us, and the answer eludes us as it eluded him. Historical method turns out to be powerless, and we perceive nothing that is surely objective concerning the inner, and even the exterior, life of Bernard.

Once again we come up against the idea of the 'mystery of Saint Bernard' which William of Saint Thierry set before us:[82] the more he talks about it, all through Book One of the *First Life*, the less clearly he seems to know it and to reveal it to us. There is a kind of apophatism analogous to the only worthwhile discourse that certain mystics have held about God, forcing us to seek what he is by saying what he is not. Hence the stress laid by William on the fact that we cannot know Bernard if we have not, like him, had an experience of spiritual realities. He aimed at presenting Bernard less as a well established historical character, situated with exactitude in a given period and place, and less as a model to imitate, than as a mystery to revere and admire, to fathom if we have received the grace to do so.

82. Cp. *S. Bernard and the Cistercian Spirit,* CS 16 (Kalamazoo, 1976) 9-11.

Chapter II

LITERARY FORMS & SPONTANEITY
IN BERNARD OF CLAIRVAUX

I. PROBLEMS AND METHODS

It is now generally admitted that a psychohistoric approach to persons of the past is possible and thus legitimate when we are in possession of sources of works penned by them or by those who knew them well.[1] *A priori*, there is no reason why this method should not be applied to medieval texts. Saint Bernard of Clairvaux, who not only wrote a great deal but was also the subject of many and sometimes lengthy testimonies offers us a good opportunity for trying out the method. The enquiry may even prove to be very broad and impinge on many areas. The historian of spirituality, for example, may wonder whether, and to what extent, spontaneity, even aggressiveness, on one hand, and the desire to create for contemporaries and posterity beautiful works of literary art on the other, are compatible with holiness.[2] Here we shall deal uniquely with the problem of the relationship between his psychic activity and the art of writing well. And even in this area, we can do no more than trace a few provisional tracks in a vast and hitherto unexplored field. An examination of the manuscript tradition of

---

1. 'Modern Psychology and the Interpretation of Medieval Texts', in *Speculum* 48 (1973) 476-490. Since then have appeared several fascicules of the review *History of Childhood Quarterly: The Journal of Psychohistory*, vols 1-3 (1973 and 1975).

2. See below, ch. VII.

Bernard's works has produced studies on their literary aspects. There are even studies on his psychology as an author.[3] The time has now come to consider his psychology itself.

Put concisely, the question is this: in his work, to what extent does literary art dissimulate or reveal the spontaneous play of his psychic processes? Anyone who examines this question carefully will find Bernard to be a very interesting, even a privileged, case. For, by his own admission and the judgement of his contemporaries and critics up to our own day, he was undoubtedly a literary man and a personality endowed with powerful psychic dynamism. As a writer he conformed to genres, submitted to laws and made use of the literary devices generally accepted in his day. But did this conformity to convention allow him to reveal the real Bernard? To take one example: like many other authors, he had a tendency to exaggerate, in the precise sense which this word has in literary tradition.[4] Did he give in to it more than other authors? And if so, why? Certainly, it is a difficult and dangerous thing to read between the lines. Certain methods attempt to do so, however, by analyzing the unconscious and the subconscious expressed on the level of consciousness.

Freud, it has been said, was a linguist. It is true that throughout his works, whether he is interpreting dreams or analyzing waking acts, he most frequently uses puns, verbal equivalences and other forms of word manipulation as indications. His method, like that of Jung, has been prolonged by linguistic analysts of several schools of contemporary thought. The unconscious and the pre-conscious are structured in language, and the mechanisms of conscious discourse at once dissimulate and reveal a certain logic or coherence of phantasms and drives. If we may approach

---

3. *Recueil d'études sur S. Bernard* 3 (Rome, 1969) 13-104.
4. See *Recueil d'études* 3: p. 50.

Saint Bernard from this angle, new light will surely be shed on his character, his style, and his interventions in the events of his day.

A first prerequisite for such a study is impartiality. This is rare in Bernard studies. It would not be difficult to demonstrate that most historians who have had something to say about him have not only judged him but have done so with a certain passion: they either present empirical impressions 'ot scientifically—or clinically, if you prefer—founded, or they transfer to him their own psychological problems. Occasionally such evaluations have been dictated by political considerations. This is particularly true of the followers of 'marxist history'. Today, however, certain historians more correctly appeal to sociological criteria which allow us to situate Bernard in the then evolving structures of the society of his day.

Indeed, a second prerequisite for objectivity is taking into account all the elements of a given culture in the area of psycho-sociology. One important element which cannot be ignored in a christian culture is faith. We begin to see something of the ever-increasing complexity of the study of multiple circumstances and an infinite variety of elements about which we possess but few documents. A few years ago, a debate between specialists about a particular moment in the history of Cluny, the abbacy of Pons de Melgueil, demonstrated how difficult, however interesting, it is to interpret—or at least to attempt to interpret—a conflict about which we have a great deal of information, but very few texts.[5]

The method we spontaneously think of applying is lexicographical. The concordance of the complete works of Saint Bernard (now completed) ought to make it possible to study his vocabulary relationed to certain attitudes which reveal his psychology. Two pit-falls immediately open up.

5. The papers occasioned by this debate are published under the title 'Encore Pons de Cluny et Pierre le Vénérable', in *Aevum* 48 (1974) 134-149.

First of all, the significant words are not those we immediately think of today. For example, that Bernard had a strong dose of aggressiveness is obvious, but the word *aggressio* is not found in his works and the verb *aggredi* is rare. When it does occur, it often has the very ordinary sense of starting to do something, for example, starting to write. Elsewhere this verb is applied to the demon who fights against man and against whom man fights back. Or it is applied to Christ, who has taken on the difficult work of our redemption. Sometimes *aggredi* is connected with the Christian's inner combat. In one instance it has to do with the attack on heretics 'by words and not by the sword'. In short, this terminology is infrequent in Bernard's works and reveals little about his psychological attitudes. We notice, however, a greater frequency of words like 'peace' and those connected with the 'social' life. This should warn us of another danger lying in wait for the lexicographical researcher, namely, the risk of examining a single group of words without considering the antonyms. John F. Benton has pointed out that an argument advanced to prove the authenticity of a work attributed to Abelard, based on the frequency of the adverb *vehementer*, as 'typical' of his style and character, is undermined by the fact that *diligenter* is found just as often but conveys a totally different sentiment.[6]

The only valid method in applying psychohistory to Saint Bernard is to work in an interdisciplinary way with medievalists, psychologists, linguists, and even physicians. The research should be conducted not over vast collections of texts or facts, but on particular 'case studies' based on specific documents. They may deal with certain of Bernard's acts known to us by his writings or by texts coming from other authors. The most explicit source will often be pro-

---

6. John F. Benton, 'Abelard's Style: A Test of Authenticity in the Correspondence Attributed to Abelard and Heloise', paper prepared for the IX Conference of Medieval Studies, Western Michigan University, 1974.

vided by one of his own works, for these present ample and varied material, ranging from 'confessions' where he describes, or mentions by way of allusion, what is going on within him, to conflicts, like those which brought him into conflict with Arnold of Brescia or Gilbert at Poitiers, to his interventions in wars and the schism in the roman Church. An entire section of the *De consideratione* suggests to Eugene III and to the curia a *revision de vie*, an exacting examination of conscience. The sermon addressed to the clergy, *On Coversion*, contains a keen analysis of an inner crisis. One of the *Sentences* describes at length a period of convalescence transposed from the physical to the spiritual plane. A long list of such examples could be drawn up. Almost everything remains to be done. Here all I can do is summarize the results of some of the research work already completed. I will then deal at greater length with some more specific problems.

II. UNREPRESSED MECHANISMS

The importance which Freud and other psychologists give certain seemly insignificant details of behavior which are in fact very revealing of unconscious drives, is well-known. This is true for style as well as for spoken discourse or 'slips'. To forget to mention a fact necessary to understanding a text or to insist on a minor circumstance for no apparent reason may indicate deep but inhibited states of soul. Freud suggested this when he pointed out a very small literary fact in his study of Leonardo da Vinci. He wrote:

> Among the entries in Leonardo's notebooks
> there is one which catches the reader's attention
> because of the importance of what it contains
> and because of a minute formal error. In July
> 1504 he wrote: 'On 9 July 1504, at 7 o'clock

my father, Ser Piero da Vinci, notary at the pal-
ace of the Podestà died, at 7 o'clock. He was 80
years old and left ten sons and two
daughters.'...The small error consists in the
repetition of the time of day 'a ore 7' (at 7
o'clock), which is given twice, as if Leonardo
had forgotten at the end of the sentence that he
had already written it at the beginning. We call
this repetition of words 'perseveration'. It is an
excellent way of stressing the affective ac-
cent.... Without Leonardo's affective inhibition,
the note in his journal must have run somewhat
as follows: 'Today at 7 o'clock my father died -
Ser Piero da Vinci, my poor father!' But the
displacement of the perseveration on to the
most indifferent detail in the report of his death,
the hour at which he died, robs the entry of all
emotion, and further lets us see that here something was concealed and suppressed.[7]

In Bernard's letters the clearest example of a similar process is provided where he 'orders'—his own word—Aelred of
Rievaulx to write the treatise *The Mirror of Charity*.[8] Bernard repeats his injunction with amazing insistency. His mis-
sive has no introductory greeting such as was customary
both for himself and other letter-writers of the period, even
in a letter-preface. Having stated twice—once positively and
once negatively— a principle of humility which precludes
any refusal on the part of the recipient, he repeats his order
with an evident tendency to dominate others and to impose

7. S. Freud, *Leonardo da Vinci and a Memory of his Childhood* (1910)
119-120.
8. This letter, published for the first time by André Wilmart, 'L'instigateur
du Speculum caritatis', in *Revue d'ascétique et de mystique* 14 (1933) 369-388,
is number 523 in volume 8 of the critical edition of *Sancti Bernardi Opera*
(Rome, 1977).

his point of view:

> I have asked you or, rather, I have commanded
> you...better still, I have summoned you.

After this he vents his aggressiveness, revealed by the
rhythm of the phrase: the stress is laid on the final formula:
'It is your obstinacy I accuse'. And the accusation goes on
indirectly in a series of questions which Bernard hastens to
answer in the place of the person he is asking. He refutes all
objections before they can be uttered and puts Aelred in contradiction with himself saying, 'Humility for you has consisted in excusing yourself; but does humility consist in not
obeying? Does humility fitly do anything but silently
comply?' The attack goes on and is followed by a repetition
of the order already given: 'I persist in my opinion, I
reiterate my command'. The style is insistent, breathless.

In the second half of the letter the tone gradually changes,
as though, having vented his repressed feelings, Bernard
calmed down. Not only did he now understand Aelred, but
he even began to 'accept his excuses, and that very willingly'. He even finds reasons for him to pluck up courage.
And in the last half-line Bernard offers brotherly love. He
began by scolding like a vexed father and ends up as a
friend.

We notice the same type of change in tone, but in the opposite sense, in Letter One addressed to young Robert, who
had passed from Cîteaux to Cluny. There too a burning
passion—love of the cistercian life—constantly surfaces in a
discourse which pretends to be inspired solely by motives of
charity. An irrepressible aggressiveness bursts out from beginning to end in the letter. At the beginning it is expressed
in terms very similar to those used by present-day
psychologists. Bernard says he is 'frustrated'; he admits he
'cannot hide his sorrow', 'repress his anguish', 'hide his
sadness'. He has been traumatized, 'wounded'—this word

occurs four times in ten lines. Throughout the letter an examination of vocabulary and style reveals a powerful psycho-dynamism whose spontaneous outbursts are not entirely controlled by the restraint which cold reason might dictate.

After giving free vent to passionate impulses in these preliminaries, even 'contrary to order and law', Bernard declares he does not want to put the blame onto anyone's shoulders (¶ 1). But he cannot help doing so immediately. At once he acknowledges he himself is certainly at fault, and adds 'let it not be attributed to you'. He repeats 'But it would as I have said, have been my fault'. Then, little by little, the fault becomes Robert's, first conditionally, then very positively and 'as many people think'. At this point Bernard is still ready to share the blame with his cousin: 'Whether my fault or, as I rather think, yours'. Yet, the fault lies mainly with Robert, who is treated like a sinner who must admit to his fault if he wants to be pardoned (¶ 2). If this fault is shared by anyone it must be by Cluny, its Grand Prior and community. Now they become the major defendants and the target of a satire conducted with perfect literary technique. Bernard brings their case to trial . This terminology is very frequently used from here on, to the point that the precise use of words shows that the accusation has been taken to the supreme court: 'I appeal to your tribunal, Lord Jesus' (¶¶ 6-7). Saint Benedict is called into the witness box (¶ 8). As for Bernard himself, he has never had, and has not even now, any feelings other than those of a mother towards his young cousin, who was once his disciple and his spiritual son. The idea of paternity is scarcely mentioned; instead we read about 'giving birth to' and 'feeding' a 'little one' with 'milk', about caressing and then 'weaning' him so that he can 'grow up'. The words which follow graphically suggest the same sentiments: *sinus, uterus, viscera*. By now Bernard is completely innocent: everything has happened through the fault of everyone except himself.

It is he who has unjustly been the victim of the kidnapping of his child, like the mother accused in Solomon's presence by a harlot. He does not even say, so obvious is it, that the supreme Judge, the true Solomon, will decide in Bernard's favor (¶ 10).

In all this, how much can be attributed to style and consummate literary art, and how much to the instinctive aggressiveness of a nature we guess to be extraordinarily rich? The same question might be asked in connection with the use he makes in the same document of terms of warfare: 'take to flight', 'lay down arms', 'try one's strength', 'return to the fight', 'struggle' like a 'soldier of Christ' in order to 'conquer' and 'triumph' over the enemy army; attack and counter-attack, the surprise of being attacked in the rear; assault on the trenches and the ramparts, rushing the least defended gate; arrows flying in all directions, sword, helmet, cuirass; help from companions in arms when surrounded by the enemy; the trumpet blast rallying the troops. All these details which we read about at the end of the letter (¶ 13) formed part of an attack on a fort and Bernard frequently applied them symbolically to the spiritual life.[9] Is such imagery merely a commonplace used by everyone in those days or was it instead a marvelous instrument serving passions which were boiling up in Bernard and which he was attempting to repress or to justify by pretending lofty motives, but which he was unable to 'dissimulate'? Among the possible images at his disposal he had made a choice and he consciously chose the themes of an accusation before a tribunal and of storming a fortress by arms. This marvelous document began by refusing to blame anyone and ended on the note of *Vae victis*: 'Woe to you—*vae autem tibi*—if, refusing to fight, you lose not only the victory but also the crown'!

In other letters written at short intervals about a same

---

9. An example is analyzed in 'Essais sur l'esthétique de S. Bernard', in *Studi Medievali* 9 (1968) 726-727.

event Bernard used such varying tones and styles that we
can detect both literary skill and the ebb and flow of an inner passion which alternately swells and subsides. We see
this in letters written between July and November 1138,
about the election of a cluniac monk to the bishopric of
Langres, the diocese in which Clairvaux lay. Letter 164,
written to Pope Innocent II, is highly satirical and reminds
us of the style of Cicero's *Pro Caio*. Bernard calmly
denounces, one after the other, the increasingly wicked
deeds of everyone not in agreement with his point of view.
The pope had given instructions, but the archbishop of
Lyons contravened them; the canons of Langres anticipated
the day set for the consecration of the new bishop and
changed the place. It is for historians to verify whether these
facts are accurate or whether, as it seems, and as Peter the
Venerable thought, Bernard paid too much attention to un-
founded hearsay. In this letter to Innocent II he treats what
he knows, or thinks he knows, as though he were writing a
police report or a business letter. He has a specific purpose:
to quash the election, and he calmly articulates everything
that could achieve this. His self-control is all the more re-
markable in that he was worn out by the fatigues of a long
mid-summer visit he had just made to Rome, where he had
done everything he could to bring the Anacletan schism to
an end, and then by the return journey from Rome. Yet under this very calculated restraint we sense his peevishness.

 Bernard's anger bursts out again in a second letter (Letter
166) to the pope. This time he is obviously irritated and
domineering. Was he merely pretending to be angry? Either
way, he is angry, he knows he is, he says he is, and he uses
his impatience to attain his ends. To force Innocent II into
action, he actually blackmails him. He starts by pouring out
a series of serious but general accusations, formulated in the
plural—'They pile on evil'—or impersonally—'Fury is let
loose'. The only crime he mentions with any precision, and
one wonders whether it was necessary to do so, consisted in

reviling the pope's name. And in this phrase curiously enough—Bernard speaks directly to the pope in the familiar second person singular rather than the more formal second person plural which he uses in the rest of the letter in formulas smacking of flattery. Could this inadvertent use of the second person singular in the violent part of the letter have been a slip on Bernard's part?

The second half of the letter is calmer in tone. Bernard begs, moans about his health, recalls everything he has done for the pope during the schism. He calls for pity, uses affective arguments. Here, as in his letter to Aelred, he seems, after a first burst of aggressiveness, to regain his self-control and feels a little guilty. He accuses himself: 'But what am I doing? I have gone too far, I confess; it is not for me to accuse anyone...'. A third letter to the pope (Letter 167) is shorter and provides nothing new: terrible but unspecified accusations; a lot of words and few precise facts. A fourth letter (Letter 169) is less personal: it is a sort of report on the latest events. Whereas throughout the preceding letter Bernard had used the second person plural in addressing the pope, here he uses the more familiar singular. Is it possible that both these letters were drafted by a secretary, perhaps even by two different secretaries, whereas the first two had been dictated by Bernard himself while he was laid up with fever, tortured by physical and moral sufferings: 'lying in bed, tortured more by the suffering of the heart than of the body' (Letter 166,2). In the space of a few weeks, we have four letters to the same person, letters which reveal contrasting states of soul of a very determined man who knew what he wanted, but had his ups and downs.

Letter 168 about the same affair reminds the roman curia of all the services Bernard has rendered its members and consequently of the right he has to their help against his enemies. Another letter (Letter 165) sent to two dignitaries of the church of Lyons, Falk and Guy, is full of bitterness. But Letter 170, written to the King of France, is clear and moderate with no trace of either anger or severity. When the conflict had been settled in the way Bernard wanted he sent another letter to the pope on behalf of Falk, who had been elected archbishop of Lyons. This and the two following letters—one written in Falk's name and the other to him—are calm. Now it is to be remarked that throughout this collection it is in the documents—consequently in the moments— when Bernard's passion was at its peak that we find the most literary artifice. In particular we notice plays on words of the most contrasting kind, for example:

non festa, sed infausta sollemnia...(Letter 164,2); *non sacramentum, sed sacrilegium* (Letter 164,5); *non sponsum, sed monstrum* (Letter 165); *non clamosis, certe lacrimosis* (Letter 166,1), as though Bernard needed to be worked up into a state of excitement or at least tension—caused by desire or some other strong feeling—to get such bright literary ideas and give the full rein to his talent. There are authors who only write well when they are angry. Were we in Bernard's case to formulate in terms of modern medicine the diagnosis drawn from an analysis of the style of these few letters, we would describe him as cyclothymic, alternating between states of depression and hypomania. We notice a certain aggressiveness of which he was conscious and which he even seems deliberately to have cultivated in the service of his chosen values but which was never entirely uncontrolled. The alliance of spontaneity and mastery of both self and the means at his disposition is undoubtedly a sign of maturity. In psychology, inhibition is said to be the root of all evil. Bernard liberates himself by expressing his feelings, and in so doing he invents those verbal consonances and conjures up from his deepest depths all those images and reminiscences which impart to his style its great vigour and color, its force and poetry.

III. EXPRESSED MOTIVATIONS: THE PROLOGUES REVISITED

In his Prologues or in the letters which serve as prologues, Bernard sets forth the intentions he had while writing each of his works—with the exception of his sermon collection— and they offer good material for studying his psychology as an author. I have already examined these Prologues to determine their conformity to literary tradition and the circumstances in which they were written. Here, I would like to discuss what they show us about the relationship between psychology and spirituality for in them Bernard was engaging in a kind of self-therapy. I shall deal simply with strictly literary themes and attempt to show the extent to which they depend on art, and thus on artifice, and to what extent they were sincere.

The most frequent theme is *trepidatio*, the fear which a writer feels in exposing his reputation to the criticism of contemporaries and posterity. The problem is already very evident in the Prologue to the 'first work', the treatise *On the Steps of Humility and Pride*. A still-young Bernard wrote this as abbot of Clairvaux at the request of his prior, Geoffrey. In the Prologue to the homilies *In Praise of the Virgin Mother*, next in date, Bernard let it be known that he was ill, isolated from his community and says that he was overcoming his hesitation. Then, throughout his career the words he uses most frequently in his Prologues suggest that he had been ordered to write, that he gave 'willing and even joyous' but never easy consent. The repeated references to the conflict between pressure from without and struggle from within, as he tried to decide whether or not to write, makes us wonder whether all this is just so much literature. And yet we know of at least two cases in which Bernard refused to comply. The first is his silence when his friend William of Saint Thierry wrote asking him to refute the errors of William of Conques. Bernard did nothing. He did not even reply to William, even though he had already com-

posed several works at his request. He also refused to give
way to Gehroh of Reichersberg, who was urging him to take
part in a dispute over the Incarnation. And whenever he did
agree to write, he left himself free to choose his own literary
genre. For example, when Eberwin of Steinfeld asked him to
refute the Cathars in the Rhineland, he did not write a special treatise but merely devoted two sermons— dense sermons, it is true— of his work on the Song of Songs to the
subject.

Each of the Prologues should be read from the
psychologist's point of view with the purpose of discerning
what Bernard really thought over and beyond what he wrote.
Here I would like simply to draw the reader's attention to
two facts constantly revealed by these texts. In the first
place, Bernard experienced an instinctive fear of writing for
the public. Secondly, he was able to master this fear when
he wanted to do so and he assumed easily the responsibility
of having some part to play. He never attempted to hide his
'timidity', his *verecundia*, this sort of inhibition which he
considered a handicap. But he also showed that he had the
strength to take initiatives compatible with his gifts and useful to his mission. The artist in him was able to reconcile the
rules governing the literary genre of the prologue with an
avowal of his limits and the demands of his deepest self.

A minor theme which sometimes crops up in Bernard as in
other writers is that of brevity: masters in the art of writing
have always recommended avoiding 'prolixity'. But for an
impulse person, for a temperament bursting with energy,
brevity is something more than a literary quality: it supposes
a control of both the need and the ability to be lavish. Yet
Bernard seems not to have had any particular difficulty in
this area: he does not mention the concern to be brief as frequently as did Peter Damian. By nature Bernard reacted
rapidly, and brevity seems to have been part of his character.

In the Prologue of his *Treatise on the love of God* he
declares that he agreed 'not to be silent so as not to seem to

be a philosopher'. This allusion becomes clear in the light of a tradition which originated among orphic mysteries and their adepts and which was given a christian interpretation by Clement of Alexandria and other Fathers of the Church. Bernard is deliberately refusing to consider himself one of the privileged few who, by their silence, keep a secret known only to the initiated. He has an inner urge to express what he feels and it is this urge which decided him to overcome his *trepidation*. In this case we have two themes, both of them literary and psychological, cleverly combined.

In the Prologue of the treatise *In Praise of the New Knighthood*, Bernard manipulated military terms with admirable ease. Was this just his way of adapting himself to the mentality of his readers, the Knights Templar, in order to secure their hearing? Or does his text reveal traces of the childhood and adolescent influence of a knightly family? In certain of his monastic texts he uses the theme of the *militia Christi* inherited from a long tradition. Can anyone unravel his dependence on patristic language, his concern for present circumstances, and the drives of a belligerent temperament? Only a thorough investigation of Bernard's conduct all his life long could answer. For the present we can only point out how very difficult the problem is.

Finally, in the Prologue to *On Consideration*, the last in date, we notice a theme which seems, through the clever use of biblical reminiscences, to betray Bernard's deep-seated attitude to Eugene III, who, before becoming pope and thus Bernard's superior, had been his novice. Bernard still considered the man to be his 'son' and he expressed the depth of his feelings by using the words 'charity', 'affection'. and especially 'love' (which occurs three times in twenty lines), and the verb 'to love' (used five times). Twice Bernard says that he still considers himself a 'mother' to Eugene and he betrays a possessive love not unlike the attitude he showed towards his cousin Robert, as we saw in the first letter of his register. Here no more than there could Bernard bear to have someone who was once part of his very substance, part of his 'marrow', torn away from him: 'You can never be separated from me: I will follow you anywhere'. So much did he love that he was well nigh 'in love'— *amans-amens*— such love can only be understood by experience: *qui vim non sentit amoris.* With this forceful formula Bernard ended his prologue. It started on a note of 'modesty', 'reverence', inspired by the 'majesty' of 'the most blessed pope' and after an irrepressible crescendo it culminates in an exasperated need to have some sway over him, to dominate him in some way. Fortunately, Eugene III managed to keep his distance, to stay free even though it meant crossing swords with Bernard. He probably guessed that his former abbot's lines were not just literature, but covered up something much deeper.

IV. AGGRESSIVENESS

Most historians have principally noted in Bernard's character the ardor and occasionally the violence with which he intervened in certain conflicts. Today we are coming to realize more clearly that many of his struggles were rooted in a very deep attachment to the cistercian way of life, particularly to the observance of his own abbey. Thus, indirectly, his efforts stemmed from his love for Clairvaux and the development of its daughter houses. This explains the rivalries not only with Cluny, but also with Morimond, another of the first four daughter houses of Cîteaux.[10] Bernard fought to defend his ideal and sought to put into key positions

10. This has been brought to light by A.H. Bredero, *Études sur la* 'Vita prima' de Saint Bernard (Rome, 1960) 63-68. The whole manuscript tradition of Saint Bernard's works illustrates, not only the difference between the 'zone of Clairvaux' and the 'zone of Morimond', but a certain lack of communication between them, as I have several times had occasion to show, for example, under the title 'Lettres de S. Bernard: histoire ou littérature?' in *Studi medievali* 12 (1971) 21, with bibliographical references.

churchmen who he knew would favor its expansion. This fact is illustrated principally by the disputes over the episcopal elections at Langres and York, and also by the discord between Bernard and Abelard who, as Bernard knew, felt more sympathy with Cluny than with Cîteaux. Bernard's psychological approach to Abelard as it is reflected in his style deserves careful study in the light of those themes which, from its inception, the Church has traditionally used in combating heretics. Something of Bernard's inmost being surfaces by means of adherence to literary rules.

Likewise, in the correspondence over the episcopal election of Langres, where Bernard arranged to have Geoffrey de la Roche-Vanneau, one of his monks at Clairvaux, not to mention his cousin, replace a cluniac monk, his 'noble style' and the absence of postal secrecy[11] probably account to some extent for the fact that Bernard occasionally uttered serious but inaccurate accusations.[12] Yet, here again, he could not help revealing his character: when he made his claim he was irascible;[13] when he had won the day he was calm.[14] His fits of anger were willed, even controlled, as means to a specific end.

Especially interesting is what D. M. Knowles has called 'The Case of St William of York'.[15] William Fitzherbert, supported by Henry of Blois, bishop of Winchester and

11. On the lack of historical precision resulting from the noble style and the lack of postal secrecy, see 'Lettres de S. Bernard: histoire ou littérature?', in *Studi Medievali* 12 (1971) 35-40; 'Limites de la valeur historique des épîtres', and 'Recherches sur la collection des épîtres de S. Bernard', in *Cahiers de civilisation médiévale* 24 (1971) 210-212: *Rôle des porteurs*.

12. For example in Letter 167. On the events, see Giles Constable, 'The disputed Election at Langres in 1138', in *Traditio* 13 (1957) 119-152.

13. Epp 165,168.

14. Epp 171,173,180.

15. David Knowles, 'The Case of St. William of York', in *The Historian and Character* (Cambridge, 1963) 76-98; this eminent historian has written, p. 76; 'It is possible to arrive at something approaching to a clear view of the whole business.'

papal legate, was elected to the see of York in 1142 and consecrated the following year. But he was immediately con-
tested by the Cistercians of the neighboring abbeys,
Rievaulx and Fountains, both of which were daughter-
houses of Clairvaux. He was deposed by a cistercian pope,
Eugene III, in 1147. In 1154, a year after Bernard's death,
he came back to York as archbishop, was confirmed in his
see by Rome, and ended by being canonized in 1226.

In order to have William deposed and replaced by Henry
Murdoch, a monk of Clairvaux, Bernard wrote seven important letters to three successive popes, to the roman curia, and
to the King of England, as well as several missives of lesser
importance.[16] In connection with events the circumstances
of which are now well-known, we have therefore a fairly
abundant file offering a field of psychological investigation.
Here I shall consider simply the processes of style which
give us an insight into Bernard's internal mechanisms.

We may reduce them to three, which we find in varying
degrees in all the texts: flattery, disapproval, and menace.
Flattery is very obvious in the last lines of Letter 235, written to Celestine II: 'I have written with such confidence because I am fully aware of your love for righteousness. I pray
that this love may never grow cold but may wax ever
warmer, most holy and loving father...'.[17] This passage has
been preserved only in letters of english provenance. Why
did Bernard discard it when he prepared for the official
publication of his letter collection?[18] Did he find he had

16. I have made a critical edition of these texts in 'Lettres de S. Bernard
trouvées depuis les Mauristes', *Sancti Bernardi Opera* 8 (Rome, 1977)
491-501, letters 525-535.

17. Edited in 'Lettres de S. Bernard trouvées depuis les Mauristes', *Sancti
Bernardi Opera* 8 (Rome, 1977).

18. This letter and those concerning the election at Langres were placed by
Bernard in their chronological sequence in his register, as I have shown under
the title 'Recherches sur la collection des lettres de S. Bernard', in *Cahiers de
civilisation médiévale* 14 (1971) 213-215.

overdone the flattery? We can ask the same question about a letter to Lucius II which is also not included in the register, and in which Bernard writes: 'I leave your judgement to decide how far the prestige of Rome has suffered in this matter. Would that the song in which they sing that Winchester is greater than Rome be silenced on their lips...'.[19] Yet in the published correspondence we find examples of flattery which are just as excessive. To Eugene III Bernard goes so far as to suggest: 'Deal with them so that they may know that a prophet has arisen in Israel...'.[20] In another letter he writes: '...so that the Church of God over which you have been placed by the Founder may see the fervor of your zeal, the might of your right arm, and the wisdom of your soul, and that all the people may fear the priest of the Lord and harken to the wisdom of God commanding righteousness through his mouth...'.[21] Those examples are only extracts from broader contexts where such words are enlarged upon. Obviously, Bernard knew the persuasive power of flattery. He aimed at touching a man's self-esteem, one which was even greater when identified with a role like that of the papacy'.

But it was when he wanted to disapprove that Bernard was most skillful in using the resources of his style. He used anything to discredit his enemies: he calls Henry of Blois 'that old whore-monger of Winchester';[22] to describe William Fitzherbert he played with words laden with disgust and fury, saying that he had not been 'consecrated but desecrated', a strong thing to say indeed. Bernard went far over the mark in repeating a story in the worst taste: 'His Eminence of Frascati who...is papal legate in this region, has (we are told) heard such tales about this man that his nostrils

19. Ed. G. Hüffer, *Der heilige Bernard von Clairvaux Vorstudien*, (Münster, 1886) p. 235.
20. Ep 238.5.
21. Ep 238.
22. Letter to Lucius II, ed. Hüffer, p. 236.

could not endure the stench of them were the power not given him from on high'.[23] These phrases and other pages in the same vein are not found in the register of letters. We would like to think that Bernard later regretted having written them. But we wonder what opinion he had of Eugene III when he wrote these letters attempting by such arguments to awaken horror against an archbishop.

We cannot help wondering about Bernard, moreover, when he applies all sorts of disgraceful comparisons to William Fitzherbert: Simon Magus, Baal and Dagon, an idol, the devil, a thief, a robber, a leper, death, a wild beast ravaging the Lord's vineyard. Are these Biblical images merely symbols and nothing more? Where did reality lie for Bernard? Had he not twisted it so much that he distorted it? Did the use of emotionally loaded symbols prevent him from seeing people as they really were?

He gave way to other greater exaggerations, until irony became sarcasm, a deviation Bernard was capable of avoiding when he wanted to. In these letters he tried to frighten the popes in order to force a value system on them.[24] According to Bernard, William Fitzherbert betrayed the value system he was defending in his moralizing and haughty way. He knew he was superior and he treated William as his inferior, and he also tried to force his point of view on the pope.

Another method Bernard used when he wanted to excoriate someone consisted in conjuring up an aversion by applying negative and off-color sexual language to them: 'People are pointing their finger at the Church's shame: Innocent has been stripped and left for the dead by a crooked servant and

---

23. Ep 239, fragment edited by Hüffer, p. 237.

24. See below, ch. III. On sarcasm as an attempt to impose a value system through fear, see R. Prentice, 'Linguistic and Value Structures of Irony', in *Antonianum* 48 (1973) 234-247.

they laugh at his nakedness'.[25] Here, flattery, irony, and sarcasm unite in an emotional appeal to the pope's self-esteem. Bernard describes the derision which the pope is inviting as a sexual offense. In yet other letters Bernard speaks of shameless fornication and humiliating nakedness.

Finally, after flattery and disapproval Bernard turned to threats. We find them in almost every letter, seriously compromising the honor not only of two popes, Celestine II and Eugene III, but also of the whole roman curia and threatening their eternal salvation: 'Take care, my Lord Father, that your heart does not incline to wickedness...for the Lord will punish you...'.[26] 'You will have no excuses...'.[27] 'How many roman pontiffs died after a short time: let this be a warning to you...'.[28] These are only a few of the many examples that could be quoted.

After reading these texts we would seem to have no alternative than to judge Bernard harshly. But that is not our point. Our aim is to discover how Bernard's style reflects his inner impulses. In expressing them, he had recourse to rhetoric. But do rhetorical methods disguise the truth entirely? For example, everything we know about William Fitzherbert from his contemporaries and from impartial historians proves that Bernard was either badly informed or else totally lacking in objectivity.[29] Moreover, between one letter to another, we find contradictions about his election. Was Bernard tricked by passion to the extent of blindness on the subject, or was he the first victim of his own facility in wielding abuse? Where in this correspondence does the boundary lie between sincerity and literature? The few ideas

25. Ep 235.2.
26. Ep 235.3.
27. Ep 236.1.
28. Ep 238.7.
29. David Knowles, *The Historian and Character*, pp. 81-82 says of William Fitzherbert: 'His contemporaries and those who wrote before his canonization agree that he was amiable and generous...'.

set out here do no more than raise the question. One thing is sure: the personality of the abbot of Clairvaux was complex. It was so filled with contrasts that it is disconcerting. And its many facets are reflected in the variety of his styles.

V. CONCLUSION: THE MYSTERY REMAINS

At the end of a solid study entitled *Myth and Science in the Twelfth Century. A Study of Bernard Silvester*,[30] Brian Stock asks, 'Literature or science?' Similar questions may be asked about many other authors and their works, probably about all of them. *The Letters of Saint Bernard: history or literature*?[31] This was the dilemma I faced after lengthy research on the correspondence of the abbot of Clairvaux. Some years earlier I had dealt with a similar problem: the connection between literature and charity in the conclusion to a chapter on Saint Peter Damian as a writer.[32] We could formulate other problems of the same kind in dealing with the twelfth century, and with Saint Bernard in particular: *Literature and the Mystical Life*;[33] literature and hagiography; literature and politics; and finally literature, psychology, and holiness. The relationship between them could well be the object of historical research in so far as objective religious values are served more or less faithfully by a man's artistic talent and character.[34] In the Middle Ages,

---

30. (Princeton, N.J., 1972) p. 273.

31. Under this title in *Studi Medievali* 12 (1971) 1-74, after having formulated the dilemma, and then examined the part that history and literature had in the letters of Saint Bernard, I concluded that it is a 'spiritual literature *a propos* of historical facts'.

32. *S. Pierre Damien, ermite et homme d'Église* (Rome, 1960) 173.

33. Title of the Epilogue of *The Love of Learning and the Desire for God* (New York: Fordham University, 1961, 1974).

34. This problem is dealt with under the title 'Psychology and Holiness', in chapter VII, below.

governed by classical and patristic literary tradition, writers were obliged to use literary genres, rules of composition, processes of expression, even at the risk of sacrificing everything else.

And yet, perhaps we are faced more with a conciliation than with a dilemma: perhaps the problem is not psychology *or* literature, but psychology *and* literature. We might say that applying psychohistory to texts is the art of reading between the lines, of discovering an author's defense mechanisms in order to penetrate his deep and spontaneous reactions beyond the literary forms in which he consciously clothed his thought and mental attitudes. The tendency to exaggerate is found in all conventional styles, but is it more noticeable in Bernard than in other writers, or more marked in some categories of his works than in others? Do we learn anything about his aggressiveness from the literary genres he chose? He was particularly fond of letter writing, manifestly, because letters lend themselves to polemic, whereas a treatise or a sermon is normally more irenic. But Bernard used all the genres. We can arrive at a fair and well-informed judgement only after careful examination of all his texts. Again, although Bernard was capable of rigorously logical thought in discussing doctrine, he sometimes contradicts himself in his letters where he reveals himself as a man of action.

We could add many other remarks of this kind and each would raise a new question about his works and his character. Nearly everything has yet to be done before we can answer them. Historical research has already greatly clarified the events in which Bernard was caught up. What we need now is a study of his language as a mirror of his psyche. Each new linguistic study on one of Bernard's texts throws new light on his mechanisms. Of course, the deep ego from which they rise, and the way in which they concur on the surface eludes us to a great extent, perhaps for ever. But at least such analysis is worth while: an enormous field of investigation is open to researchers.

Chapter III
MECHANISMS OF IRONY

I. AN APPLICATION OF PSYCHOLINGUISTICS

The science of linguistics is constantly making progress and is taking increasing interest not only in the analysis of texts as such but also in the ways they were produced and consequently in the ways in which they should be read. It aims at discovering the personal reactions of the author. This is particularly true of transformational grammar, also called generative phonology, which studies the process of sentence formation and all that this implies of optional elements—for example, the addition or deletion, the inversion or suppression, of words—which may occur within the limits of certain obligatory rules governing sentence formation in any given language. These free syntactic structures reveal the deep structure of a phrase underlying its surface structure.[1] In examining these we grasp, over and beyond what the author writes about the events, the psychological structures—the unconscious mechanisms, the motivations—which moved him to write and which were operative in him as he worked.[2] In this way they help us to evaluate the ob-

1. R.H. Robins, *A Short History of Linguistics* 2 (London, 1969) 228-229; the pages which follow, 230-233, retrace the history of this discipline and provide a bibliography on the subject. Application in English has been made by, among others, Roderick A. Jacobs, Peter S. Rosenbaum, Paul M. Postal, *English Transformational Grammar* (London, 1968) *passim* (the *Index*, p. 294, at the word *Transformation* and its derivatives indicates many passages of the book where it is mentioned).

2. Milka Ivic, *Trends in Linguistics*, translated by Muriel Heppell (La Haye-Paris, 1970) p. 206; bibliography pp. 210-211.

jectivity of a work and, especially, to come to a better knowledge of the author himself. It is now accepted that this psycholinguistic approach to texts has a contribution to make to theology,[3] to the study of politics,[4] and history,[5] medieval history included.[6]

Of course, it is not easy to apply to the past psycholinguistics as it is generally practised: the dead cannot be summoned to the laboratory. Nevertheless, certain laws are common to the ways both ancient and modern writers express themselves—laws ruling language and style, the written and the spoken word—because in all cases we are faced with 'verbal behaviors' taking place in the making and the perception of language. In other words, we are faced with the intellectual and emotional attitudes implicit in a given communication. Normally this requires the testing, classification, and interpretation of spontaneous phenomena. This research should also take into account linguistic

---

3. This is testified to by the colloquium whose proceedings have been published under the title 'Analyse linguistique en théologie' in *Recherches de science religieuse* 61(1973) 5-51, with bibliography.

4. This has been shown for communist vocabulary, for example, by the works of Annie Kriegel, especially *Communisme au miroir français* (Paris, 1974). See also L.J. Calvet, *Linguistique et colonialisme* (Paris, 1974).

5. A method of application of linguistics to history has been proposed by R. Robin, *Histoire et linguistique* (Paris, 1973) but the author makes only rare allusions to the Middle Ages (p. 63) and they are mainly in citations of Marx (p. 97) and Engels (p. 99). There are examples from the Middle Ages in Nancy S. Struever, 'The Study of Language and the Study of History', in *The Journal of Interdisciplinary History* 4 (1974) 401-416.

6. Under the title 'A Socio-Linguistic Approach to the Latin Middle Ages', in *The Material Sources and Methods of Ecclesiastical History*, Studies in Church History, 11, ed. Derek Baker (Oxford, 1974) 69-82, Michael Richter deals not with linguistics, but with 'the linguistic situation' in the Middle Ages. But in a paper presented at the Ninth Conference of Medieval Studies, Western Michigan University, Kalamazoo, Michigan, May 1974, under the title 'The Failure to Mobilize Public Opinion: Propaganda and Lyons II', Charles W. Connell has shown what all the linguistic analysis of documents contemporary to the second Council of Lyons (1274) can provide for our knowledge of the way in which people then tried to fashion public opinion.

anthropology, that is, those cultural events which have conditioned communication and which in some way make up the background, the historical context.[7]

In view of all that has just been said, it seems legitimate to apply psycholinguistic methods to a twelfth-century author like Bernard of Clairvaux. However, in this field, generalities are not enough. Nor, is it possible, at least at the outset, to put an extensive literary production through the fine sieve of minute analysis required by this type of research. Consequently we may rightfully, and we must, restrict our study to texts illustrating one or another specific linguistic and psychological structure. In the following pages we shall consider one of those structures which recurs frequently in Bernard's works: irony. We do so from the point of view not of general psychology,[8] literary history,[9] or theology,[10] but from that of the mechanisms which it brings into play in its attempt to convey a veiled truth and

7. Cp. Ivic, pp. 170-171.

8. V. Jankelevitch, *L'ironie ou la bonne conscience* (Paris, 1950) has studied different varieties of the movement of the ironic conscience, such as pretence, parody, cynicism, from this point of view. R. Mehl, *Les attitudes morales* (Paris, 1971) has spoken of everything opposed to the 'serious': humor, laughter, smiling, joking, mockery.

9. Sister Geraldine Thompson, *Under Pretext of Praise. Satiric Model in Erasmus' Fiction* (University of Toronto Press, 1972) 185-191, has provided a bibliography on satire and irony. Stephanie Ross, 'Caricature', in *The Monist* 58 (1974) 285-293, has studied the connection between these two means of expression: drawing and language. At the Ninth Conference of Medieval Studies, (Kalamazoo, 1974) Frederic Amory gave a paper on 'Irony and Ironists in Antiquity and the Early Middle Ages' (*Abstracts*, Session 39). See H. Newstead's review of D.H. Green, 'Irony and Medieval Romance', in *Cahiers de civilisation médiévale* 17 (1974) 176. Green's article studies five sorts of irony in romance literature and appears in D.D.R. Owen, *Arthurian Romance. Seven Essays* (Edinburgh-London, 1970).

10. William F. Lynch, SJ, *Images of Faith: An Exploration of the Ironic Imagination* (University of Notre Dame Press, 1973) has applied the categories of irony to the 'epistemology of faith' and to Christ. Cf *Le rire du Seigneur. Enquêtes et remarques sur la signification théologique et pratique de l'ironie biblique* (Strasbourg, 1955).

make it acceptable.

Robert Prentice has studied several authors who use irony as a form of literary art. In particular he studied what he called the 'yes/no mechanism wherein the language we actually use becomes the means of denying what we say in order to say what we do not say...in order to communicate to the hearer (or reader) exactly the opposite of what we are saying'.[11] Prentice has shown that this form of irony includes the following elements: 1) a linguistic structure; 2) a semantic context; 3) a 'context of communication' between the speaker (or writer) and the hearer (or reader), some sort of complicity between the person who is being ironic and his partner who he supposes will agree; 4) a value context common to both. In short, irony requires a shared context.[12]

The elaboration of these various givens into good and effective irony is a work of art: 'Irony as discourse lies within the competence of every man, but only the gifted can create a genuine aesthetical experience in themselves and in their hearers in their actual performance while using irony. For here the element of free choice enables the performer to sufficiently escape the determinism of the structure and flee the structure of predictability through art'.[13]

'True irony can function solely as a vehicle of positive value judgement. Negatively toned lexical items can be used to carry only favorable value content'[14] concerning the realities being dealt with. Otherwise it becomes sarcasm, and offensive to the listener. It uses violent means to arouse fear in the listener by putting him in a position of inferiority. By using verbal violence, irony exerts a psychological pressure and forces the outward acceptance of what judgement in-

11. Robert Prentice, 'The Linguistic and Value Structure of Irony', in *Antonianum* 48 (1973) 235. I am grateful to this author, now deceased, for having helped me in preparing the present essay.

12. *Ibid.*, p. 239.

13. *Ibid.*, pp. 241-242.

14. *Ibid.*, p. 243.

wardly refuses. The simulated truth presented in irony becomes offensive, hurtful, and easily injurious.[15]

Saint Bernard used irony. But what kind? Did it turn to sarcasm? Was it offensive or unjust to those it addressed? When a text is 'published', as are the works of Saint Bernard, the recipient is no longer merely the person or persons to whom he wrote and who he assumed shared a context with him and consented to values they had in common; it is also his unknown readers. Are they going to understand, to receive the text in the same way the original reader did? There is no general answer to such questions. We must examine specific texts with minute analysis, the description of which is bound to be dry. Things would be different in a seminar. There we would accept prolixity in exploring often dense texts. Among the different texts we could select for our study let us take some which reveal the different aspects of irony: a treatise on good monastic observance; a letter sent to a young cleric to sting his conscience; a series of caricatures meant to illustrate the demands of a single virtue, humility.

II. IRONY IN CRITICIZING THE CISTERCIANS

The *Apologia to Abbot William* contains a series of invectives against the Cluniacs and is a model of satire. It is only normal that we should immediately think of using it to study Bernard's use of irony.[16] It makes its first appearance at the beginning of the first part of the treatise, after the introduction on the lawful variety of monastic observances. It is entitled *Against detractors*. These detractors of then-traditional

15. *Ibid.*, pp. 244-247.
16. The text is in SBOp 3 (Rome, 1963) 81-108. On the *Apologia* as a model of the literary genre of satire, see *Recueil d'études sur S. Bernard* 3 (Rome, 1969) 45-54, 81-84.

monasticism, in particular the Cluniacs, were the Cistercians. Bernard aimed to bring them down a peg before attacking the Cluniacs.

First of all—*primo*—he fires off nine questions in which he affirms what he wants his readers to deny or else denies what he wants them to recognize as being true. For example: 'Does the Rule not accord with the Gospel and the Apostle?' The answer can only be 'of course it does', because this is a value common to both writer and reader. Had the answer been 'The Rule does not accord with the Gospel', there would have been no further room for discussion.

To stress this common value, the ground of his whole argument, Bernard used satire. It consists in exaggeration by a series of contrasts in which the interlocutor is brought into contradiction with himself: 'In tunics and self-sufficiency we disdain furs...' (Apo 12). Bernard is making a positive statement in order to provoke a denial: 'No! We don't do that'. In this compact sentence, which he later develops, Bernard opposes tunics and self-sufficiency just as humility— symbolized by the tunic— is opposed to pride. Tunics and furs are contrasted as are simplicity and luxury, symbolized by furs. Tunics and self-sufficiency are in opposition to 'we disdain'. If furs are disdained through pride, then the very thought provokes a sort of gut reaction. We find the same procedure in the next sentence: 'What is more, with our belly full of beans and our mind puffed up with pride, we condemn those who stuff themselves with food'. The final part of this paragraph is a series of contradictions which call up more contradictions. In this way Bernard makes the thinker advance step by step until he eventually comes round to agreeing: two negatives make a positive. We may wonder how fortuitously Bernard inserted into the context, in connection with a biblical allusion to the 'waters of contradiction' (Num 20:6, Ps 77:15-21), the word 'contradiction', which is typical of the psycholinguistic structure he was using.

Through the medium of style, Bernard was stating explicitly everything that is implied under the surface of satire. His aim was the acceptance of a well-defined value system: to over-eat is wrong, but to be proud is worse; it is right to disdain luxury, but to condemn it for a wrong motive is evil. The art of satire lies in knowing just how far one should make explicit the value system one is trying to convey by exaggeration. In satire truth is not denied but exaggerated in such a way as to gain acceptance of the unexaggerated truth. The art is to know just how far a contrast can be set up between what is exaggerated and what is not. The satirist presents nothing new but merely appeals for the recognition of what already is. Saint Bernard exaggerated the non-value of over-eating in order to win acceptance for the value of moderation. Had he overdone, or even underdone, his exaggeration, the manifest untruth would have been rejected by the interlocutor who, would have refused to respond to the appeal and not have acknowledged the truth. On the other hand, when an interlocutor is faced with the happy medium, the right measure of exaggeration, he willingly recognizes and accepts the truth conveyed by the objective untruth exaggerated. Then the tone gradually changes: exaggeration gradually drops away and satire—a negative form of irony—gives way to positive discourse. In this way Bernard goes on to justify his use of irony (¶¶ 13-14), arguing that the spiritual vigor of the Cistercians, shown by their physical mortification, is not to be tarnished by pride and uncharity. He continues to pose questions but now in order to give his own positive answers borrowed from Holy Scripture. These become, as it were, a channel—*fistula* , a favorite word with Bernard— through which all his conscious energy flows. Here, as in many other arguments he puts forward, biblical allusions and reminiscences lead to direct quotation.[17] Bernard seems to fade into the background, yielding to the word

17. Examples in *Recueil* 3: 202, 204-205, 240-241, 260.

of God which it was his sole aim to introduce: Scripture acts as a catalyst forwarding the chemical reaction between two bodies but remaining itself unchanged.

At the end of this first section (¶ 15), aimed at the Cistercians, a clever opposition between scandal and truth—inserted as a caveat from saint Gregory—serves as a transition to the virulent attack Bernard was about to launch against the Cluniacs. It paves the way for the 'scandal' he is about to denounce. From the point of view of style everything that has so far been said by Bernard prepares the reader for the second section: *Against excesses*.

III. IRONY IN THE SATIRE AGAINST THE CLUNIACS

Again we have from the beginning a series of oppositions forming a keen existential description of the monastic virtues and the dialectic which sometimes is set up between each one and its caricature:

abstemiousness	is accounted	miserliness
sobriety		strictness
silence		gloom;
or, in the opposite sense:		
laxity	is labelled	discretion
extravagance		generosity
talkativeness		sociability
laughter		joy.

Bernard goes on in the same vein for several lines.[18] In each instance the 'material object' of a virtue, that is, the practical action by which it is manifested, is opposed to its 'formal

18. We find same procession about the same realities in Ep 1.4 (SBOp 7 [Rome, 1974] 29-43). There Bernard reproaches his cousin Robert for having gone from the observance of Cîteaux to Cluny.

object', the intention behind the act. This leads Bernard to one of his strongest affirmations: 'This sort of kindness is full of cruelty...'. It is cruelty to take care of the body and to kill the soul it should serve.

What follows shows immediately that Bernard and his readers shared a value system without which his argument would have been meaningless: 'What mercy is there in feeding the servant girl and killing the mistress?' For Bernard it would be merciless to care for the maid and kill the mistress. Nowadays we should be inclined to think that the maid has as much right as her mistress to live and that it would be unlawful to kill either. But Bernard and his contemporaries— at least those for whom he was writing—accepted a social system which saw nothing wrong with ill-treating servants, and indirectly he is even approving of it. Today, the very idea of comparing a lady and her maid shocks us, for the notion of mastery and domination suggest alienation, a lack of humanity. But for Bernard this symbol had not yet lost its significance and he had every right to use it in this context.

In the following paragraph (17) he clearly articulates the contradiction conveyed by the contrasts mentioned above:

it is not	mercy	but	cruelty
	love		ill-wishing
	discretion		disorder.

This is all put together so harmoniously, orchestrated so musically that the reader—who is also a hearer, because he reads aloud—is disposed to give his attention to the rest of the satire. Bernard's art lies in his ability to coordinate three levels of expression: the syntactic, the phonologic, and the semantic. We may, of course, wonder whether and to what extent Bernard, in this and in so many other pages, was aware of these processes we detect by psycholinguistic analysis. Yet on the other hand, is it not characteristic of the creator, the poet, to produce beauty spontaneously, without being aware of it and, we might almost dare say, without doing it purposely? A writer who is merely a good grammarian or even a philologist would attempt it in vain. The creative wealth of a genius like Bernard springs from the depth of his inner dynamism, which is beyond the surface level of which he is aware. And he finds this deep, intense human experience in Holy Scripture, and appropriates it to express his own inner experiences in texts where the vigor of his psyche, the rigor of his art, and the loftiness of his religious inspiration are fused into one.

These first paragraphs of the second section of the *Apologia* make up a general introduction to his denunciation of a series of eight abuses which are described in the subtitles, and may be authentic, that is, dating from Bernard himself.[19] They concern the excess attributed to the Cluniacs in food, drink, mitigations in the diet accorded healthy monks, superfluous or superb attire, the inattentiveness of superiors, the pomp of their entourages, the sumptuous decorations in monasteries. These reproaches were probably justified to some extent but they are quite obviously exaggerated. Yet they were well received by those to whom Bernard was writing[20] and the *Apologia* was widely diffused in traditional monastic circles. This is shown by the manuscripts[21] and can be explained by the psycholinguistics of irony. Bernard used irony but stopped short of sarcasm, though sometimes only just in time, on the borderline. He knew that both Cistercians and Cluniacs wanted truly to be monks; this was their shared value system. The Cluniacs recognized themselves, at the deep level of their vocation, under the surface structure of satire which, though it came very near to caricature, sprang from the clear-sighted fervor which inspired Bernard to pinpoint deviations which are al-

---

19. Cp. SBOp 3: 75.
20. Cp. *Bernard de Clairvaux* (Paris, 1953) 193-203, 490-503.
21. In SBOp 3, I have indicated the manuscripts.

ways possible and were, in this case, partly true.

IV. IRONY AND AFFECTIVITY IN THE LETTER
TO FULK OF AIGREMONT

Among the texts where Bernard uses irony we find Letter Two written to a young man named Fulk.[22] Bernard battered him with questions: more than sixty in a few pages. But the issues raised by this letter are more complex in that we are no longer dealing with a large group of anonymous monks, as in the *Apologia*, which gave Bernard a chance to describe a monastic ideal in contrast to these monks' way of life. Here we have a specific individual, a member of well-defined family and clerical class. Consequently, before analyzing this text we must briefly recall the sociological and historical facts necessary for understanding it.

In, or shortly before, 1120 Fulk of Aigremont, having already been professed in a house of Regular Canons, left religious life and joined the ranks of the secular clergy. That was why Bernard wrote him, to reproach him for being unfaithful to his vocation by giving in to pressure from his uncle, Vilain of Aigremont. The uncle, fairly old by this time, had been named a canon of the cathedral of Aigremont thirty-six years earlier, in 1084; in 1099 he became an archdeacon and was dean of the chapter from 1106-1111; from 1125 until his death in 1136 or 1137, he was bishop of Langres.[23] Both he and his nephew were Bernard's cousins.[24] In addition to these family ties with Bernard, Vilain had connections with the Cistercian Order because of the part he had played in the foundation of the abbey of Morimond,

22. The text is in SBOp 7 (Rome, 1974) 12-22.
23. See Damian Van Den Eynde, in J. Leclercq, *Recueil d'études sur S. Bernard* 3 (Rome, 1969) 364, and *Bernard de Clairvaux* (Paris, 1953) 635.
24. *Bernard de Clairvaux*, pp. 119-122; the genealogical tree is give on p. 121, note 25.

whose charter he had drawn up.[25]

In his letter to Fulk, Bernard writes: 'Even to this day, this uncle of yours has resisted the Holy Spirit with all his might. He even wanted to damp out my fervor as a novice but, thank God, he was not able to do so. He has also greatly persecuted his other nephew Guerric, but in vain: this young man stood his ground and became more glorious by this trial' (Ep 2.3). But with Vilain's intervention Fulk did well and in 1125, five years after Letter 2 was written, the uncle was appointed bishop of Langres and the nephew was named archdeacon of the same diocese. Against this background of family relations, ecclesiastical promotion, and monastic politics—especially those concerning Morimond, Clairvaux's twin sister and rival[26]—the letter to Fulk must be read.

To describe what determined the psychological mechanisms of this letter, we may use the linguistic schema of transformational grammar by which one moves from a deep to a surface structure. In the generative process leading to an uttered surface statement, the performer draws upon an unconscious creative process in which his personal experience is submitted to the orderings of the syntactic level of semantics and finally materialized in the words of spoken language on the outward phonological level. The process is completely unconscious—at least in what concerns the ordering of the syntactic and semantic elements— and it can be detected only with the help of a theory which endeavors to explain, or to explicate how it comes about.

In a parallel way, even if it is not a direct experience of spoken language, there is a generative process giving structure to this letter, in which Bernard moves from a deep level to its surface expression. The progression discernible in this letter as it passes through the stages of this generative proc-

---

25. *Ibid.*, pp. 132-133 and p. 284.
26. See L. Grill, 'Morimond, soeur jumelle de Clairvaux', *ibid.*, pp. 117-146.

ess is connected with the unconscious which underlies its wealth of meaning. It can only be explained at the cost of complex and subtle analysis. We may distinguish a sequence of five levels.

The first level appears in the letter's opening paragraph. We come up at once against surface irony: 'I am not surprised that you are surprised that I should wish to write to you, a bumpkin to a man about town, a monk to a schoolman, when there seems no reason for this' (Ep 2.1). The surface irony here is a cover for Bernard's conviction that he and his cousin Fulk are not indifferent to each other. Bernard was conscious of his love for Fulk and knew that the young man accepted not only this love but in turn sincerely loved Bernard and admired his work in founding Clairvaux. It was this acceptance of mutual affection which made it possible for Bernard to use irony, with some hope of success, at the beginning of his letter. He unwittingly banked on this affection when he set out to write. This unconscious choice, disguised as friendly irony, opens the way to a clearly-worded expression of affection. This is still somewhat stilted, couched in literary terms like 'Oh good mother, charity' rather than in really personal words. But the link between what this formula says and Bernard himself is so evident that irony is only a gentle way of evoking the mutual love existing between two people who are too delicate, too refined, to mention it openly.

Generative grammar or, if you like, the study of the linguistic process of thought, helps us to see that under this surface irony lies a real affection imperfectly expressed by irony. Since it is present at the beginning of the letter it is now possible for Bernard to glide, perhaps unknowingly, from the language of irony to that of love.

On the second level, in the first paragraph, we notice a double process of linguistic generation. In a first phase Ber-

nard attempts to draw Fulk's attention to the conscious and
the unconscious elements behind his decision and the consequences it will have. In a second phase he appeals to their
mutual affection in order to soften anything hurtful in this
suggestion of unconscious motivations for he thus touches
the most sensitive and vulnerable spot of any personality.

Let us first of all examine Bernard's appeal to his cousin's
unconscious. Bernard explicitly asks Fulk to examine his unconscious motivations. He does so by a play of words difficult
to translate. He mentions 'the charity which sorrows over
you, even though you yourself are not sorry; which is moved
by your misery even though you are not miserable'. On the
surface, in other words, Fulk is not upset: he does not perceive how miserable he is. By addressing him in these terms,
Bernard is asking not to pause at this superficial level where
everything seems to be running smoothly, but to go down
into his heart, there where he really lives, and to determine
his true state: he is neither sorry for himself nor self-pitying,
though he has every reason to be for, in spite of what he
thinks, his plight is sorry and pitiable: 'whereas you are to
be sorrowed over, you are not sorry...whereas you are a
misery, you are not miserable'.

Bernard was treading on dangerous ground here because
Fulk, deep down, knew that he had done wrong and that he
alone was responsible; he knew that if he did not admit his
fault he would be inwardly divided against himself and that
this was against nature. He was well aware of all this even
though he did not let it be seen on the surface level. He
knew equally well that the very core of his personality was
being challenged: what he accepted in the present would determine his whole experience. Naturally, Fulk realized quite
fully that his unconscious worms its way to the surface when
he expresses his conscious thought and he saw quite well
that he was being invited to accuse himself to make his own
self-criticism as we now say—and this is never a pleasant
thing to do—and to go back to a life of penance and self-

sacrifice. In the relatively easy life which was now his, however, it was not easy for him to look this alternative in the eye.

Bernard had touched the most sensitive area of Fulk's personality at that very place where his ideal was its most elevated and his capacity for self-fulfillment its richest. But the young man found the words by which his cousin invited him to sorrow over his plight and to admit his need for pity, very difficult to swallow.

At this level, too, the linguistic form of irony had given Bernard—though he may not have realized it—the means of reaching the most sensitive point of Fulk's personality. Irony is indirect and deliberately ambiguous: it speaks truth under cover of untruth. In this way it is possible to shift from the ambiguities of linguistic discourse to the ambiguities of inner motivations. This possibility is inherent in the very nature of discourse. We have here a case where we can almost literally say 'deep calls to deep' (Ps 41:8). The deep of an ambiguous truth calls to the deep of ambiguous feelings. The transformation of deep structure gives rise to a surface structure.

Yet, Bernard softened his appeal to Fulk to be severe with himself by his indirect expression of affection. He knew that only affection would affect, if we may say so, Fulk's unconscious motivations. Quite likely he realized that his affection gave him a right to enter the most intimate realms of his cousin's soul.

Bernard did not explicate the psychological structures underlying the structures of his discourse: both language and discourse passed through the matrix of those awarenesses which made Bernard the man he was. Even less conscious was his decision to appeal to affection through the indirect language of irony.

The way Bernard wrote made it obvious that he felt obliged to appeal to affection in order to get down to the level where Fulk really lived. Yet his way of writing showed too that personal affection was not the only emotion to enter forbidden territory: it was accompanied with objective, universal love, charity personified, 'good mother charity'. Fulk could accept that and in this way love entered his unconscious, helping heal it. Bernard found the friendliest path leading Fulk to conscious avowal of a truth which he had so far kept hidden on the instinctive, almost fierce, level of his unconscious. By thus indirectly mentioning love Bernard himself was guided by the unconscious pressure of his own deep structures. These are not at all evident; we get no more than a fleeting glimpse of them. But we may at least, with the help of methods proposed by generationalists and transformationalists in linguistics, point to pathways by which his language came to the surface.

There is still another fact determining Bernard's unconscious choice of the indirect form he used. His unconscious mechanisms urged him not only to formulate an indirect appeal to love but even led him to describe this love as mother love. Charity could have been described as 'divine' or as the working of the Holy Spirit; it could have been called 'brother' love or anything else, but no! it was 'mother'. Who can say what inner riches in Bernard's unconscious dictated this choice? It may be imagined that it stemmed from a keen intuition that he let him 'figure Fulk out' as it were, and to love him with so insightfully and so aptly.

Taking the few facts we know into consideration, we might be led to think that Bernard's surface level choice was determined by those deep structures which had inspired his instinctive appraisal of Fulk's personality: he had been drawn away from his vocation by his uncle, a member of the clergy, and not by a girl of by a desire for freedom or by laziness. It is not insignificant that it was his uncle who had led him astray for this implies a maternal relationship, the most basic, existing between a maternal uncle and his eldest niece. In the case at hand the family tie existed between a nephew and an uncle, and even were he to be an uncle on the mother's side, nothing would be explained. What interest other than an affective one would an uncle have for Fulk? What Vilain offered his nephew was the opportunity not of carrying on the family name but of inheriting a church benefice. The few facts we know lead us to think that Fulk was a refined young man with delicate tastes, in no way given over to the vulgarity of natural appetites. He had no ambition to marry and no desire to found a family, but he does seem to have wanted to persevere in the clerical life and to accept the modest responsibilities of an archdeacon of Langres. Perhaps, Bernard detected in him someone strongly marked by some sort of oedipus complex. Whatever the truth about this, he seems unconsciously to have had good reasons for appealing indirectly to mother-love.

Third level. Having pierced through to Fulk's psyche and been accepted, Bernard was now in a position to make a direct appeal that he look his personal psychological and spiritual situation squarely in the face. Having worked his way into this *sacred domain* by means of affection clothed in the literary form of a mother, Bernard knew, by reason of some sort of structure urging him in his depths, that he could go still further and ask Fulk to listen honestly to the description of the state he was in. Bernard's move is structured evenly at different levels.

1) *An appeal to honesty as regards courage.* It was useless for Fulk to hide behind the pretence of having been strong-willed in leaving the regular canons and of having given demonstrated independence in judgement and action. With vigorous irony, Bernard says that Fulk was merely seeking the easy way out: 'You are inexcusable.... Your uncle asked you, he did not bind you; he drew you by attracting you but he did not drag you by violence. Who forced you to believe this man who attracted you, to consent to the man who was drawing you?' (¶ 2). This is nothing but a sign of

weakness, it can be rectified on the spot. But if this weakness is camouflaged as courage it begins to be so dangerous that it may be well nigh incorrigible. Unconsciously and without being in any way explicit, Bernard was urged by his deep structures to put this terrifying danger to Fulk. 'You have not been strong', he says, 'but weak. Others thought to be your inferiors showed more strength than you: in me too, they once wanted to damp out the fervor of a novice but, thanks be to God, they did not succeed. Another uncle strongly resisted his nephew, but in what way was he able to harm him? Are you stronger or more prudent than he?' (¶ 3)

2) *The truly crucial level of this drama* is that of the attractions which, literally, rule Fulk's psyche. Bernard, with no explicit reasoning process, puts this to Fulk quite plainly saying that he has been overcome by an attraction which is very like a woman's seductiveness. If Fulk had really given himself to the Lord he would have had no interest in anything anyone set before him to lure him away: 'Now, having already once given up the world, ought you to have followed a worldling?' (¶ 2) ...Had he had the mind of Christ, he would not have been so grieved according to the flesh but would rather have rejoiced in the Spirit. But because he found the things of this earth more savory than those of heaven, he was troubled and sad...' (¶ 5). People who really want something know instinctively how to avoid whatever threatens it. A sheep does not let a wolf rest upon its breast, a dove does not invite an eagle to shelter under its wings. If Fulk could be attracted, it was because he wanted to be. This is very strong language on Bernard's part, but it had the desired effect on Fulk's judgement, whatever it may have done at the level of his emotions and his decisions.

3) *What has been done cannot be undone but it can be reintegrated.* Bernard was an utter realist when it came to someone's honesty about his deepest personality. What Fulk

had done remained a fact and had to be considered as such: 'What has been done can no longer be un-done; what has been heard can no longer be kept hidden' (¶ 5). It would be better for Fulk to look what he had done in the face and be honest about the consequences of his decision rather than to try to hide behind specious excuses: 'Let honesty now give way to utility and shame to necessity. I prefer sparing the timidity of a young man to seeing him overcome by wretched sadness' (¶ 5).

The fourth level is that of Fulk's responsibility. After all this groundwork Bernard placed the entire business at the very center of consciousness. He had wanted to do this at the outset but he had had to prepare Fulk to accept conscious responsibility. He now lays the whole blame on him: 'Your fault is grievous and your fall wretched...' (¶ 8). Fulk alone is responsible for his present state and for everything he had brought about, by his own choice, in his spiritual life.

The final level is the one that counts most. Bernard, in rich terms, and vigorous sentences, exhorts Fulk to understand the gravity of everything he has done. Bernard's aggressiveness here is transformational, and thus creative. Fulk is informed that he had indeed seen the work of the Lord and that if he now rejects such a precious treasure, he rejects everything for which Christ died. He falls from a lofty vision of truth because he has been lured by his own weakness, his irresoluteness. Fulk must now try to understand that he has put himself in the same position as Eve when she lost the vision of the tree of life and desired something less good.

We may point out that part of Bernard's irony is expressed in military terms which have today lost their meaning as an incentive to self-conquest. But in the days of knighthood and crusades such language was acceptable. Yet, we cannot help

asking ourselves whether this was really an effective motivation to propose to a young man like Fulk as Bernard describes him.

Whether or not its imagery was really appropriate, Bernard
continued to use it and he built to the climax of asking Fulk
to acknowledge Christ as Christ, that is to say, as the ulti-
mate reality by which he will be judged as he really is: 'I
beg you, let yourself be known before, let yourself be seen
as you are.... If Christ knows you now, he will acknowledge
you in heaven...so that you may say in all confidence: 'Then
I shall know as I am known' (¶ 12). We are now at the highest level, the level which determined the composition of this
letter from beginning to end.

V. CONCLUSION. IRONY AND CHARITY

In Bernard's writings irony appears in other forms than
those which have just been described; these too are worth
studying. In particular we notice that satire occasionally becomes something very akin to caricature. Generally, when
we speak of caricature, we think of means of expression
having to do with the representation of images meant to be
'seen' through the medium of pictorial or graphic plastic art.
But the aim of caricature can also be attained by writing. As
the word itself shows, caricature— derived from *caricare*,
meaning in Italian, 'to charge'— is always an exaggeration
accentuating to the extreme or even to excess certain physical or character traits of someone who is thus held up to
ridicule; others smile or laugh at him but they also get an
image of him which is generally opposite his real normal
image. In this case caricature is related to the yes/no structure of irony. Because it is facilely partial, showing only one
side of men and things, it readily becomes unjust and unkind
and tends to make people despise what it describes. Pushed
to the limit it is not only comic but grotesque. If used

kindly, however, and with charity, it can be one of those forms of educational humor of which medieval literature, and Saint Bernard's works in particular, gives us so many examples. Everything depends on an author's ability to discern just how far he can go without being offensive. If this discernment is made at the outset, then the fun, the *divertimento* of caricature can be legitimately aggressive, poking fun at someone without hurting him. In this way it can be pressed into service for polemical or propaganda purposes to advance some ideal.

There is no dearth of caricature in Saint Bernard's works: we think of his description of the 'knights of this world', in contrast to the Knights Templar in his treatise *In Praise of the New Knighthood*. Similarly, in the second part of his treatise on *The Steps of Humility and Pride*, after he has treated the doctrine, he gives twelve examples of proud people in several profound and often entertaining pages. We see there that Bernard was very much a realist, gifted with a keen sense of observation but also respectful of persons. It was not particular individuals who could be recognized and named that he held up to ridicule, but groups, types of people, and this leaves each of his readers free to think that he does not fit into these categories. In fact he rarely—if ever—describes a borderline case that matches an individual. It has been pointed out, for example, that when Christ satirized the Pharisees, he was not attacking any pharisee in particular, but pharisaism in general. His direct personal contacts were always courteous. We could apply to Bernard's caricatures what the Rule of Saint Benedict recommends in the programme laid down for the abbot: 'Let him hate vice but love the brothers'.[27]

We see then that Saint Bernard used the structures of irony. By the study of its linguistic mechanisms we are able to grasp the forms his aggressiveness took and to formulate

27. *Rule of Saint Benedict*, 64.11.

the question of possible connections between his psychology and his spirituality. On the psychic level, irony seems to have been natural to him. To get an idea of its frequency, we would have to note all the texts where it occurs. But even without doing that, we can see that his inspiration in writing his first masterpiece, *On the Steps of Humility and Pride*, was not simply a youthful reaction. We find irony again at the end of his life in the cutting words he wrote in criticism of the roman curia in Books Three and Four of *De consideratione*. And yet this clear-sighted and infinitely accurate denunciation of abuses which must, at least partly, have existed has not prevented the book's popularity with popes and their entourages throughout the ages. It is true that his pages of caustic criticism are followed by a positive programme illustrated by a probably utopian description of what the pope's collaborators should ideally be. Here too, people could recognize themselves. Someone like Wycliff, who quoted the *Consideration* extensively in his attacks on the papacy retained only the texts which are, to use Saint Bernard's word, 'destructive'. Yet Bernard had no intention of destroying the papacy: he simply wanted to reform and in this sense to 'edify', to build up. He used his style to serve his purpose and saw in irony merely one way of expressing his charity.

Chapter IV

BERNARD THE PSYCHOTHERAPIST

In undertaking a psychological study of Saint Bernard we are tempted to look first of all at those sometimes violent conflicts in which he took an active part and which made him famous in monastic, ecclesiastical, political, and doctrinal history. There is no doubt that this side of his character is worth studying. Yet there are other sides which did not reveal themselves when he was dealing with adversaries but came on only in his relations with friends. This does not mean that he had no conflicts with friends, but they were of a different kind and often we do not easily recognize the Bernard we found in other circumstances. Here I would like to consider the relationship he had with two friends for whom he was a counsellor and even, to some extent, a psychotherapist.

I. RELATIONS WITH WILLIAM OF SAINT THIERRY

Bernard's best friend was William of Saint Thierry, some five years his senior. He died in 1148, that is, five years before Bernard himself, after having been benedictine abbot of Saint Thierry, near Reims, and then a cistercian monk of Signy. Their friendship was set within a conflict which arose between the supporters of Cîteaux and the supporters of Cluny. The documents concerning Bernard's relationship with William includes the letters they exchanged and Book I of the *Vita Prima*, which William wrote towards the end of his own life. If we are to believe what this text tells us—and on this point there is no reason to doubt it—Bernard and

William first met in 1120.[1] The ailing Bernard was twenty-
nine years old and William thirty-four. A few years later
when Bernard sent letter 86 to his friend, he was in a position to write: 'I know everything about you'.[2] Twenty years
later, when William wrote about his first visits to Bernard
and the conversations they had together, he reinterpreted all
these events.[3] Though he was older than Bernard, he was in
some way affectively dependent on him, and Bernard, with
his natural need to dominate and command, to be a superior,
seems to have accepted this inequality, this somewhat childish attitude in William.

Letter 86 is a short letter. The second half begins with a
health bulletin which could hardly be more vague: 'I have
been ill and still am, neither more nor less than usual',
writes Bernard laconically. This in itself was a lesson because William was impatient to have news not only about
his friend's health but also about a fugitive monk of Saint
Thierry whom Bernard was sending back. The letter also
refers to William's wish to resign as abbot and to go and
live at Clairvaux. Did Bernard perceive that this intent,
though rooted in an aspiration to the cistercian observance,
was not entirely free of a certain attachment to himself?
Whatever the case, he did his best to dissuade William from
resigning. He said that they must both ignore or, more
precisely, give up any desire to live together. He does not
deny, still less repudiate, this deep friendship. But it must always be submitted to God's will. The last lines of this note,
which insist on William's difficult duty to stay where he is in
order to be useful, are full of plays on words and assonances:
Tene...tenes, mane...es, metuis...refugis, prodesse...praeesse,

1. According to Stanilaus Ceglar, *William of Saint Thierry. The Chronology of his Life...*, Diss., Catholic University, Washington, D.C., 1971 (Ann
Arbor, Michigan, University Microfilms) 40.
2. SBOp 7 (Rome, 1974) 223-224; written before 1124, according to
Ceglar, p. 72.
3. See above, ch. I.

praees...potes, praes...prodes, praesse...prodesse. The writer of these words, who was also the spiritual counsellor, seems to have wanted to soften the harsh lesson he had just given by using literary devices. And in fact, it was only much later, in 1135, that William left Saint Thierry to enter, not Clairvaux as he first wanted, but Signy, a foundation of Igny which was itself a daughter house of Clairvaux.[4]

But in the preceding letter (85), written in 1125, Bernard reproached William.[5] Why? The gist of the reason he gives is, 'You say you love me more than I do you'. William complained about this state of affairs, said it hurt him and offered proof. 'When people here go to see you, they bring back no token of your favor or your love. I have written to you several times, and you have never answered'. The accusation was quite specific and Bernard was obliged to reply. He did so with an extremely keen psychological and spiritual analysis of both William and himself. First he speaks to his correspondent (¶¶ 1-2) then to God (¶¶ 2-3). After that he turns back to William and gives him a bit of practical advice (¶ 4).

His opening move was to turn his friend round to facing himself and to looking squarely at his intentions, the deep and unconscious movements of his soul. Bernard upbraids William for being too ready to judge himself without knowing himself and also to judge others without really knowing them. This forces William to self-examination and clear-sightedness. He is then led to query his own statements and the intentions he had attributed to Bernard: 'God alone knows the secret of hearts; how can you pretend to this knowledge? Out of a very doubtful impression you have of a situation you state something as a certainty'.

Bernard goes on to be gently ironic about his friend's certitude, in

---

4. The date has been established by Ceglar, p. 167.
5. SBOp 7: 220-223. The date is fixed by D. Van Den Eynde, in J. Leclercq, *Recueil d' études sur S. Bernard* 3 (Rome, 1969) 403.

which he sees an illusion or even, as he does not hesitate to
say, an error. In one of his clever plays on words, juggling
the sense and the sound, he moves from *forte* to *certus*. This
last word in different grammatical forms recurs eight times
in four lines, notably in that compact phrase where Bernard
tells his friend outright 'I am certainly certain that you are
not certain of what you say—*sed certe certus sum certum
non esse tibi*'. And at once, as he usually does, Bernard, who
cannot teach without referring to the word of God in Holy
Scripture, quotes numerous examples of biblical characters
who doubted themselves: Saint Paul, Saint Peter, the disciples, David. Cleverly contrasting these biblical figures and
William—'But you' (*tu vero*)—Bernard could bring in a precise and cleverly prepared reproach: 'You are too confident
in your own judgement'. Indirectly, charitably, and politely,
but barely cloaked, Bernard points out in William a lack of
something he does not hesitate to call 'maturity': 'I thought
your wisdom had attained sufficient maturity to do without
my letters'. Then under cover of another scriptural text—
Saint John's commandment to love not in words but in deed
and in truth—Bernard asks William when he had ever failed
to prove his friendship by his 'deeds'. Thus in the first part
of his letter Bernard places his friend before his own conscience and his personal responsibility and then brings him
around to querying his intentions correctly and finding for
himself the answer that. he does not want to impose by
authority.

In concluding this first part of the letter Bernard again as-
sures William of his friendship and reminds him of the
proofs he has given. Then he examines his own conscience
as William had asked him to do. To do this he puts himself
in God's presence and prays. He asks to be loved only in
God—an indirect reproach to William. Then with God as his
witness, he begins a subtle game destined to show who of
the two, Bernard or William, loves the other more. With a
didactic modesty intended to awaken a similar attitude in his

correspondent—without in any way imposing on or tutoring him—Bernard agrees to be the one who loves less. He admits that though he is less worthy of being loved, it is William who shows the more love. This leads him to pray. He asks to look clearly into himself and to be able to order his charity. He humbles himself for all that is still imperfect in him, in his intentions and in his friendships. This is another discreet lesson for William.

In concluding, Bernard talks to William again and no longer to God. He has just asked God for the grace to love. Now he says that he loves as much as he can according to the grace he has received. But he also accepts his limitations and protests against William's idealized image of him. This must have happened more than once, and we see Bernard react—with penetration and humor—in Letter 87, against the exaggerated idea that Oger had of him. William wanted to find God in Bernard. Let him think again! Let him accept Bernard 'as he is and not as he dreamt he was to be'.

A letter of this kind gives us an idea of the psychological niceties and the elevated spiritual quality of a written or spoken dialogue between friends of this calibre. It tells us something too about Bernard's intuition. He discerned that in William's friendship there was something which, while in no way unhealthy, was not entirely ordered and controlled. Discreetly and very delicately he gave him a sort of therapeutic consultation.

If the two letters which we have just analyzed betray a certain affective dependency on William's part, Bernard shows that he, in his turn, is intellectually dependent on William, who persuaded him to intervene against Abelard and his errors in 1140. Letter 327 from Bernard to William and his letter—treatise *Against the Errors of Abelard* prove that the abbot of Clairvaux, who could be so personal and independent, on this occasion trusted his friend blindly and almost excessively.[6] One wonders whether William, in summarizing Abelard's teaching for Bernard, was entirely objective. However that may be, the fact remains that Bernard trusted him. On yet another occasion when William urged him to refute the doctrine of William of Conques, he preserved his freedom of action and did not follow up.[7]

Thus the friendship between Bernard and William was complex. The friendship was certainly real and was situated on a very high plane. If either of the two partners found it difficult to remain at this level, it was William and not Bernard. Bernard led the dance, so to speak, even though William was senior in age and his equal in abbatial rank, and even the head of a monastery with more prestigious past than Clairvaux had. Yet although this friendship was spiritual it did not for all that cease to be very human. Here, as on many other occasions, we get a glimpse of Bernard's need to dominate, and his friend quite spontaneously accepts this. We may wonder whether Bernard could have been close friends with someone less dependent on him. We cannot say, but in Letters 85 and 86 to William, he states principles of detachment applicable to both of them. He could do therapy work, as it were, with William because he had first done it with himself.

If we have any right to consider Bernard as a psychotherapist, it is in the sense that he did spiritual therapy. He was more concerned with intentions, problems of conscience, than with psychological problems. What counted in his eyes were intentions, the faithfulness of each person to himself and to God. It was, so to speak, a committed, and not an impersonal, therapy because he was involved. If he tried to be impartial this does not mean he was

6. 'Les formes successives de la lettre-traité de S. Bernard contre Abélard', in *Revue bénédictine* 78 (1968) 100-105, and 'Les lettres de Guillaume de Saint Thierry à S. Bernard', *ibid.*, 79 (1969) 375-382.

7. 'Les Lettres de Guillaume de Saint Thierry', pp. 382-391.

indifferent. He did not hide his reactions as the psychiatrist does sitting out of sight of his patient, lying on the sofa talking about himself. He was moved, stirred, became eloquent and even started writing. He used his talent, duly controlled, as well as his passions in the service of the spiritual consultations he provided in his letter to William and many another.

II. WITH ANOTHER FRIEND, AND WITH HIMSELF

One of Bernard's longest letters is Letter 87, written to Oger, a canon regular of Mont-Saint-Eloi near Arras and someone with whom, from 1124 onward, he kept up a regular correspondence.[8] Several documents in this file have been carefully listed and dated by Damian Van Den Eynde.[9] The letter which interests us here is the last of the series in date: written after 1140.[10] At the outset of his literary career Bernard was urged to write by Oger, who admired his works, and, so to speak, launched his career.[11] But at the date this letter was written he was at the peak of his prestige and his influence: many others than Oger were praising him, congratulating and encouraging him to produce and to perform more and more. Oger became an abbot in 1126 and resigned his charge in 1140, retiring to the monastery of his profession.[12] From Letter 87 we gather that he had asked Bernard's advice and that Bernard had counselled him to remain in his

8. The text of Ep 87 is in SBOp 7: 224-231.

9. 'Les premiers écrits de S. Bernard', in J. Leclercq, *Recueil d'études sur S. Bernard* 3: 349-355, 377-379, 398-403.

10. On the chronology of this letter and of the series of which it is part, see Van Den Eynde, p. 378. On the reasons for which, in his *Corpus epistolarum*, Bernard regrouped letters of different dates dealing with the same subjects or the same people, see 'Recherches sur la Collection des lettres de S. Bernard', in *Cahiers de civilisation médiévale* 14 (1971) 210-217.

11. The texts are cited and commented in SBOp 3: 65-74, and *Recueil* 3: 19-20 and 37.

12. On the career of Oger, see Van Den Eynde, p. 378.

abbatial charge, advice which Oger did not follow. Now he
was suggesting that Bernard draw up a life project for him.
Apparently he wanted to give Bernard one more opportunity
for showing his talent, the quality of his teaching, now that
he had attained full maturity, and was in complete possession of his literary skill and theological thought. At the end
of Bernard's letter we find an odd text which we shall now
look at. In it the abbot of Clairvaux likens himself to a juggler and an acrobat—*ioculator, saltator*—who walks on his
hands with his feet in the air, drawing everyone's attention
and laughter. First we give a translation of these lines on
juggling even though in the process they lose much of the
charm which comes from those word plays and 'biblical
games' in which Bernard excelled:[13]

> Truly, what a great danger it is to hear someone
> say about you things which go beyond what you your-
> self feel about yourself. Who will grant me[14] to be
> worthily humbled among men for things that
> are true, in the same way that it is granted me to
> be unworthily exalted for things which are un-
> true. Then rightly would I make my own that
> prophetic word: 'being exalted I have been
> humbled and troubled'[15] and this word too: 'I
> will play and make myself despised'.[16] That is,
> I will play a sport so that they make sport of
> me. A good sport which infuriated Michal and
> delighted God. A good sport making men laugh
> but causing angels to rejoice.[17] A good sport, I

13. On the way Bernard 'plays' with scripture and on the meaning of this
play, see examples in *Recueil d'études* 1: 302-304, and 2: 254 ff. Here in the
footnotes, we will identify quotations and biblical reminiscences in the text.

14. Ps 54:7.

15. Ps 87:16.

16. 2 Sam 6:22.

17. Allusion to 1 Cor 4:9, cited further on.

say, which makes us a reproach to the rich and despised by the proud.[18] For truly, in the eyes of men of this world what else do we seem to be doing if not playing, when everything they long for in this world, we on the contrary flee, and what they flee we long for, as is the way of jugglers and acrobats who, head down, feet up, stand or walk on their hands, contrary to human ways, drawing all eyes to themselves? This is no childish sport, nor is it a play-scene stirring the lusts with dirty and effeminate antics or sordid actions. It is a pleasant, honest, grave, respectable sport delighting the eyes of heavenly spectators. This chaste and religious sport was played by him who said 'We are made a spectacle to angels and to men'.[19] In the meanwhile let us also play this sport, so that men may make sport of us, and that we thus be humbled, confounded until he comes,[20] he who puts down the mighty and exalts the humble,[21] he who will rejoice, glorify and exalt us for ever.

How does this text fit in with the long letter to which it forms the conclusion? In the opening lines, in the greeting which serves as an address to the message, the abbot of Clairvaux, a 'churchman' as he has been called,[22] calls himself an ordinary 'monk, but also a sinner'. On most other occasions he presented himself as an abbot. But already before him, and he was probably aware of the fact, another great reformer of the Church and of monasticism, Saint

18. Ps 122:4.
19. 1 Cor 4:9.
20. 1 Cor 11:26.
21. Lk 1:52, 1 Sam 2:7-8, etc.
22. As, for example, in the title of the book *S. Bernard homme d'Église* (Paris, 1953).

Peter Damian, even after he had been created cardinal, nearly always spoke of himself, in some way defined himself, as a 'monk, sinner'.[23]

Throughout the first paragraph (Ep 87.1). Bernard wrote ironically about both himself and his correspondent, but particularly about himself: someone who once refused to follow his advice now consults him as 'a teacher and matchless master, whereas if he teaches something about which he knows nothing, then it will become evident that he is ignorant'. He has come to the wrong person, trusting someone who knows he is no more than a fool (*stultus*). This very forceful word is blurted out. Bernard uses it again further on. The beginning of this letter draws our attention to the difference between appearances— by which men usually judge—and the "heart"—which God alone knows. The difference between what appears outwardly and what goes on inside, hidden from sight. No one knows a man better than he knows himself, at least if he is free from illusions, and this need for true self-knowledge is one of the most important points in Bernard's teaching.[24]

From the beginning this letter is rich in assonances and subtle word plays. In paragraph 2 and throughout the letter we find rhymes, parallelisms, plays on words juggling both sound and sense. Bernard no sooner described himself as *stultus* than he applied to Oger quite the opposite words. Oger who is 'wise' has asked advice from a fool, even after having thought things over carefully. Once advice had been given, he considered 'even more thoughtfully' that he would do just the contrary to what he had been advised. Bernard could only rejoice over this because 'each time his opinion is preferred and followed' he is burdened with the weight of responsibility, and he must wait with fear and trembling for

23. *S. Pierre Damien, ermite et homme d'Église* (Rome, 1960) 242-243.
24. 'L'expérience de soi dans S. Bernard', in *Aspects du monachisme* (Paris, 1968) 263-269.

events to show whether he was right or wrong.

He goes on to say, not without a certain irony, 'I congratulate you...' and with ironic play on words he adds that he fears that in exoneration, Oger had dishonored himself (¶ 3). Bernard's style is refined and pleasant, but his reproach is none the less hard: Oger 'did what he liked'; the verb *placere* occurs five times. Did Oger have the right to prefer his own will to the service he rendered his brothers by being their abbot?

All this may be fiction, for we now find Bernard encouraging his correspondent (¶ 4): he preaches hope and joyful fear of the Lord, virtues which will arm him against despair. The tone is set by words which speak of hope and hopefulness. Bernard stresses the ambivalent nature of all things: the pastoral responsibility and of doing what one pleases; the fear which can be either futile or a source of joy. The solution lies in humility, which lets us discern what is best.

In the next paragraph Bernard denounces the subtle pride which lies in wait for Oger if he resigns his abbatial office, the complacency which can overtake someone who thinks he has done something great (¶ 5). Bernard contrasts true humility and vain glory: 'Artificial humility introduces real pride into the heart'.

Only true penance, one that is neither deceptive nor fruitless, allows us to avoid these dangers inherent in all ambivalent things (¶ 6). Penance alone solves the apparent contradiction which Bernard translated by a string of subtle paradoxes: 'In keeping with the two fears I pointed out above, I want you both to fear and not to fear, to presume and yet not presume; to fear so you may repent, to be fearless that you may be presumptuous; to be presumptuous so you are not wanting confidence, and to lack confidence so you do not slumber'.

We have to be capable of severe self-reproach, able to direct irony at ourselves and to accept being checked on by other people. For indeed, 'to set oneself up as sole authority in matters of self-judgement is to become the disciple of a fool'—the word crops up once again (¶ 7). If to the experience we have of ourselves we can add what other people know about us, if we are able to mistrust ourselves enough to trust the judgement of others, then we may possibly 'reconcile prudence with humility'.

Bernard goes on to praise Oger for having come back to where he left, to the community to which he once belonged (¶ 8). But even that is not without danger: in the spiritual life project he traces, vigilance has a place of honor: 'Pay attention!'

Little by little the letter moves to a close. And the conclusion contains yet more instruction. For, at the point when Bernard becomes ruthless in exposing the illusions besetting all human beings, he no longer speaks as though he is giving others a bit of good advice. He becomes the target of his own irony: 'There then is the wisdom of this eloquent and elegant master you have consulted from so far away', says he to Oger, with a play on words. He goes on to say that this master is 'full of words and void of sense' (¶ 10). The public should be warned of his lack of competence. Bernard himself was well aware that, in complying with his friend's request, he had produced a work of minor importance, not a great one, and he plays on words meaning 'masterpiece' and 'minor work', and ends this paragraph with an affirmation of the 'limitations of his knowledge'.

Progressively he seems to lead his discourse, in a cleverly studied crescendo, to an even stronger declaration of his own foolishness, his total self-contempt and his entire trust in God. He speaks of the 'consolation he finds to his confusion' (¶ 11). He uses the word *stultus* again, but this time goes even further and gives his phrases cutting edge: 'Some people will mock me as being foolish, others will laugh at the idiot I am....'. But there is a choice to be made between humility and utility—notice the play on words. Humility is the key word to all that has so far been said. It is repeated six times here in the words humiliation (three times), to humiliate, and humble. Bernard then states the great axiom: 'Humiliation is the path to humility'. This is followed by a practical application: "Since people have so often praised me unjustly because they did not know me well, it is useful for me to be sometimes covered with confusion on account of those who know and thus to be brought back to just self-knowledge. That is one of the ways we avoid bragging and being fooled by one's own works."

The letter could well have ended there, for a vast spiritual teaching, something much broader than a life project for Oger, had been set out in depth. Yet in reading it we have the feeling—in line with the process of forewarning so familiar to Bernard[25]—that he had something else he wanted to say, something which appears suddenly, as though the curtain is raised on one last tableau: he spins off the scene with a pirouette. But even this clownish exit is sublime, in spite of Bernard. We have now come to the last paragraph (¶ 12), already quoted above, where Bernard likens himself to an acrobat. He begins by stating the difficulties of remaining humble amidst praise. Then the tone rises and becomes lyrical. After an exclamation ('Truly, what great danger') and a question ('Who will give me...?'), the succession of sentences in praise of play, each beginning with the words 'A good game' resounds as a hymn to play. The key-word is 'sport', used seven times, together with the verb 'to play', 'he played', 'I will play' and followed by 'so that they may make sport of me'. The finale opens out on a vista of eternity: the great game—one would almost dare say the big circus—begun here below will go on forever.

Thus, in this long and magnificent letter, Bernard not only

---

25. 'Le cheminement de la pensée biblique de S. Bernard', in *Studi medievali* 8 (1967) 4-7: 'De la reminiscence à la citation. Prélibation biblique'. There is an example of this progression in Ep 87.12, quoted above; the allusion to I Cor 4:9.

complied with his friend's request—even though he denies it throughout—but he also provides on the specific and fundamental theme of true self-knowledge and self-esteem, a teaching as delightful as it is shrewd. Bernard did not content himself with merely setting down for one more of many retired abbots a line of conduct which he could have found in many other works if perchance he needed it. Nor did he simply react against the praises of which he was the object: he had already done that elsewhere and just as delightfully.[26] But his teaching on the theme 'know yourself', which he had treated previously in different literary genres[27] he proposed here playfully, with exceptional keenness and insight. How lucid is his discernment, how pitiless his pursuit of every form of self-complacency! And yet, what gaiety, good humor or just simply, what humor![28] And with that what style! What unity of inspiration, theme, and vocabulary! How many formulas of admirable depth, only a few of which, alas, have found place here! Truly, Oger, who had formerly snatched the *Apologia* from Bernard's hands even before it was finished,[29] and who showed such constant interest in his writings, had once more drawn a masterpiece out of him.[30] In

26. Epp 18, 72.1, 123, and others.

27. In particular in the *De gradibus humilitatis et superbiae*, especially ¶ 13-18 (SBOp 3:26-30), and SC, 35-37 (*ibid.*, 1: [Rome, 1957] 248-255, and 2: [Rome,1958] 3-18).

28. 'A l'école de S. Bernard. De l'humour à l'amour, in *Témoins de la spiritualité occidentale* (Paris, 1965) 264-287, and 'Actualité de l'humour', in *Le défi de la vie contemplative* (Gembloux-Paris, 1970) pp. 264-265. [Translation of *Le défi* is projected by Cistercian Publications as *The Challenge of the Contemplative life* -ed.]

29. See SBOp 3: 66.

30. The fact that Bernard recognized Oger as a stimulant could explain his adding, at the time he published his letters, a list of his works at the end of letter 89, written to Oger—something not found in the first draft of his letter at the date it was sent. See 'Lettres de S. Bernard: histoire ou littérature?' in *Studi medievali* 12 (1971) 4-5. On letter 87, see *ibid.*, pp. 70-72, where the importance Bernard gave to this letter is shown. It is apparent in the care with which he revised the text before publishing it again in his

reading this text he surely felt the same thrill of joy we do. He has every right to our gratitude.

As always, Bernard had the knack of being original. He had his sources, or at least predecessors: all those who expounded the themes of the 'fool for Christ'[31] and the 'idiot'.[32] But it seems that he draws on Scripture alone—fairly abundantly, it is true[33]— and with his usual sovereign liberty. With supreme discretion too: he is well aware that the words 'they may mock' which he applies to himself are very similar to what the Gospel says about his Lord during his passion: 'They mocked him'.[34] But he was careful not even to suggest this glorious parallel directly. He contented himself with likening himself to David, dancing before the ark of the covenant and being mocked by Michal; and he refers explicitly to Saint Paul. He quotes the example of David elsewhere in connection with the third degree of obedience which is to obey 'with a smile', in a passage where the word 'hilarity' occurs twice and 'hilarious' thrice. Once, this last is matched with the words 'wisely': 'See David before the

---

collection of letters. As is proved by the apparatus of the variants in the critical edition, he made very many corrections to his first text, about one a line. They are nearly always betterments of detail, aiming at making the text more elegant, euphonic, tighter, more beautiful in every way. In one only case did he suppress a sentence, which, in fact, added nothing: in ¶ 2, he had first written, instead of *nec debeo indignari, indignari nec debeo, sed cuilibet de qualibet re consulenti me quod mihi visum fuerit consulo ut sapientioris non praeiudicem consilio.*

31. Texts in D. Mollat - A. Derville, 'Folie de la Croix de Dieu', in *Dictionnaire de spiritualité* 5 (Paris, 1964) col. 635-650.

32. Texts quoted by G. Oury, *'Idiota', DSp*, fasc. 48-49 (Paris, 1970) col. 1242-1248. On the use and the meaning of *idiota* in patristic literature, see also *Thesaurus linguae latinae* 71 (Leipzig, 1934-1964) col. 221-222, and 'L'Idiot à la lumière de la tradition chrétienne', in *Revue d' histoire de la spiritualité* 49 (1973) 289-304.

33. The references to the quotations and reminiscences have been given above, nn.14-21.

34. Mt 27:29, 31 and 41; Mk 15:20, 31; Lk 22:63, 23:11 and 36.

Ark playing hilariously but wisely repressing the indignation of his proud wife: "I will play and make myself meaner still in the eyes of the Lord"'.[35] There again humble juggling is contrasted with 'sad arrogance', the pride which puts on gloomy airs.

Mabillon used two words to describe the balance and subtleness of Bernard's teaching in Letter 87: *Argutum et sapiens* (pithy and wise). In a learned note[36] he suggests a comparison with the *philautia* of the ancient greek philosophers, which attracted the attention of many an author from the Fathers of the Church to the writers of the seventeenth century. Now we have on this delicate subject of 'self-love' a delightful and still timely book: Fr Irénée Hausherr has skillfully described this extremely ambiguous sentiment which can be just as much vice as virtue.[37] When it is vice it just one of the numerous manifestations of selfishness; when it is virtue it consists in 'knowing oneself as one is', mistrusting self and blaming self.[38] This attitude, which has always and everywhere been cultivated by monks, is the only condition for loving self without vanity and it prevents self-love from becoming self-esteem, ferreting out every form it may take. Then detachment, freedom from self, opens the heart to that charity which allows us not only to seek God in contemplation, but also 'to enfold in our loving-kindness those very people we would be most inclined to exclude, enemies or simply the people whom we do not like';[39] selfish *philautia* is replaced by *philotheia* and *philodelphia*[40] the main quality of which is 'universality'.[41]

35. *De diversis* 41.6; SBOp 6/1 (Rome, 1970) 248-249.

36. PL, 182: 215-216, n.264.

37. *Philautie. De la tendresse pour soi à la charité selon Maxime le Confesseur* (Rome, 1952).

38. *Ibid.*, pp. 10, 16 and *passim*.

39. G. Couilleau, 'Accusation de soi dans le monachisme antique', in *La vie spirituelle* 166 (1967) 309-314.

40. Hausherr, *Philautie*, p. 113.

In his own way, Bernard in his Letter 87 wrote a treatise of *philautia* as a virtue and it is easy to see why he insisted it be included in a selection of his best letters, in the 'register' whose publication he carefully ensured.[42]

Juggling as a profession was despised, especially by clerics. To call someone a juggler was to hurl a stinging insult.[43] Bernard inflicted this humilation on himself. But, we may ask, did not some of his contemporaries with whom he had connections use the same language, and is it not comparable with his? The teaching contained in Letter 87 on virtuous *philautia* seems timeless, not linked to real circumstances, apart from the question asked by Oger, which is no more than a pretext. As we have seen, Bernard replies partly beside the point, shifting the emphasis of the problem: instead of saying much about the conduct of a resigned abbot, he takes pleasure and delight in defining the limits of self-esteem, in instilling indifference to what people say and to being laughed at. One wonders whether Bernard did not have some real reason for saying all that. Was his reputation in danger? Were people laughing at him? Could it be that he was laughing at some of his contemporaries?

At the time when this letter was being written, Bernard was caught up in a very active controversy: in 1140 the trial of Abelard at the council of Sens was being prepared, held, and followed up. In this controversy each accused the other of childishness, even of playing the fool. A little later on, another quarrel blazed up in which Cluniacs and Cistercians

---

41. *Ibid.*, p. 112.

42. On this careful work of the edition of Bernard's letters, see the articles cited above, nn. 3 and 23.

43. Texts and images in '"Ioculator et saltator." S. Bernard et l'image du jongleur dans les manuscrits', with illustrations, in *Translatio studii. Manuscript and Library Studies honoring Oliver L. Kapsner O.S.B.*, (Collegeville, 1973) 124-128.

clashed, and here again we find the theme of playing.[44]
From all this we know that during these years Bernard did
not receive only praise and approval: and soon his reputation
was once more going to be put severely to the test when he
was held responsible for the failure of the second crusade
and its appalling consequences. Bernard had long been the
object of criticism, perhaps only by a few but not always
without cause and he knew it. Certainly he suffered from
this. There is in his style often a sort of impishness which
reminds us of Mozart and makes us think of a juggler. Yet
this playfulness covered serious feelings or, more precisely,
it provided a way for Bernard to reveal his feelings by giving them a spiritual sense and value. He acted, or believed
he did—in any case, he said he did—with upright intentions.
It did happen, but only rarely, that he changed his mind and
acknowledged his mistakes. In Letter 87, in face of the in-
comprehension of which he was the victim, indirectly and
without saying so, and also without losing his good humor,
he reaffirmed his detachment from his reputation and his
attachment to God. And he taught us all how to stay in this
frame of mind. In the course of the various disagreements in
which he was involved, the opponents readily called each
other jugglers. Bernard reversed the argument and applied it
to himself with charming precision, transforming the insult
into a religious paradox. And so it is that this letter en-
lightens us about his spiritual teaching and his attitudes to
the historical events of his day. The greatness of Saint Bernard lies in his ability ironically to refer to himself as God's
acrobat.

44. 'Le themè de la jonglerie chez S. Bernard et ses contemporains',
in *Revue d'histoire de la spiritualité* 48 (1972) 393-398.

Chapter V
INTENSITY OF INNER CONFLICTS

Geoffrey of Auxerre who had known Bernard well, had attended a number of his sermons—and not just copied out the written version—testifies to his tendency to be radical: Bernard wanted people to be either hot or cold, not merely lukewarm.[1] He himself felt everything very intensely. To understand this, we should examine his attitudes in some of the 'affairs' in which he was involved.

I. CONTRADICTIONS OVER THE MORIMOND AFFAIR

And we start with one of the first conflicts in which he was caught up: the conflict brought about by Arnold, cistercian abbot of Morimond.[2] With a group of monks he had gone off to found a monastery elsewhere. Bernard opposed this project and insisted on Arnold coming back. But Arnold had permission from Rome. He died on the way to Palestine.

It was to him that Bernard first sent his Letter 4, which reveals something of both his psychology and certain ideas generally accepted in his day. At the start he mentions the great sorrow which Arnold's decision had caused all his friends. Apparently with no respect for Arnold's personal liberty in taking this step, Bernard reproached him. The first

---

1. Quoted by Ferruccio Gastaldelli, *Ricerche su Goffredo di Auxerre. Il compendio anonimo del 'Super Apocalypsim': Introduzione ed edizione critica* (Rome, 1970) 156-157.
2. On the events, see *Bernard de Clairvaux*, pp. 125-133; and above chapter II, 2.

reason he gave was that Arnold, in leaving the monks who had stayed at Morimond, had abandoned them as sheep without a shepherd. The responsibility of those who had left with him is not even taken into consideration. It is as though they did not count; they are simply identified with Arnold. This implies that the abbot is irreplaceable and that the monks have only a secondary role to play. This made it all the easier for Bernard to exert psychological pressure on Arnold, first by flattering him as 'one of the pillars' of the Cistercian Order, then by accusing him of not having consulted the other abbots, and of letting himself be surrounded by young monks and, probably, letting them influence him. Bernard did not deny that his intentions were good—unless this is just a literary concession. At the end, he offered to mediate in order to obtain an even-rounded decision: he was opposed not to Arnold's leaving but to the way he left. In this letter Bernard's motives were good to the extent that, in keeping with the ideas of his times, he was anxious about the spiritual welfare of the monks for whom Arnold's presence was indispensable. He showed in the situation, a certain sense of observation and even a certain insight. But there is not the slightest empathy for Arnold himself: Bernard made no attempt to 'feel with' him his reasons for deciding to leave. What counted for Bernard was that Arnold return and thus restore the objective situation he considered normal.

The letters written about the same affair after Arnold's death are very different. Bernard speaks at length of him in the longest of these letters, the seventh, written to Adam, one of the monks who had left with him, and also in the sixth letter, sent to the archbishop of Cologne. In this letter he had some very harsh words for Arnold who, he says, did not act for Christ but for himself, choosing the best monks to go with him, and so on. What is the origin of this difference in the motivations attributed to Arnold and in those of Bernard himself? In Letter 4 Bernard had said that Arnold was one of the pillars of the Order and now he found nothing good to say about him. Unconsciously he distorted the facts because he wanted Adam to come back. To achieve this he had to calumniate both Adam and Arnold, otherwise the archbishop of Cologne, to whom he was writing, would not intervene to force him to return. Bernard wrote with the intention of convincing the archbishop. But did he not project on to Arnold the anger he felt himself because of the resistance which he took to be disobedience? He made no attempt to discern, by fair criticism, the justifiable elements in Arnold's decision; he refused to see anything good in his motives. Did he have any proof to justify this judgement? Is it possible that some defence mechanism led him to contradict himself in distorting the truth? For, if all that he now wrote about Arnold were true, he ought to have been pleased about his leaving and considered it a blessing for both his monastery and the Order.

The same sort of unconscious reaction appears in Letter 7, addressed to Adam. At the beginning, Bernard stated that he did not want to assess Arnold, who was now dead and whose cause concerned God alone. But this objective, serene attitude is soon followed by irritation. Arnold is accused of having dispersed his flock, troubled the peace of his community, behaved like a robber. All this provides fresh contradictions in what Bernard said. To be sure, he gives some justification of these abuses found in the second part of the letter: in order to bring Adam and his companions round to obeying, he wanted them to understand just how guilty their abbot Arnold was. But what right had Bernard to have recourse to unlawful means—calumny in particular—to obtain an end he considered lawful? Moreover, there is a contradiction between the conduct for which he reproached Arnold, Adam, and the members of their group, and his own conduct when monks come to Clairvaux from other monasteries. He reproached their departure as downright bad, decided upon without permission, in contradiction to the cistercian institution and opposed to the good of its members. The permission given by the pope made no difference, for, in asking it, Arnold was motivated by a wrong intention, and the pope had either been deceived by lies or else had given way to importunity. The monks who followed Arnold contravened their vow of stability, considered more important than their vow of obedience to their abbot. On the other hand, when monks from other monasteries wanted to settle at Clairvaux, Bernard inquired into the reasons for taking them in and he conceded that it was not easy to see clearly. He attempted to answer the question—not very convincingly, it is true— by saying that God is everywhere and that those who wish to be saved have the right to transfer to a more fervent monastery. This letter ends with a sort of prophetic threat, uttered in God's name: those monks who come back will live, the others will die. Underlying this whole argument is the conviction that the life lived in the Cistercian Order and especially at Clairvaux bears importantly on the glory of God and the good of all mankind, almost as though outside Clairvaux there was no salvation.

These are the facts that can be drawn from Bernard's letters. It is clear that we cannot judge the whole affair solely on his evidence. We need to hear the other party, to learn from Arnold, Adam, and the others what their motives really were. But can we glean something about Bernard himself, over and beyond the conscious reasons he gives for his interventions? First, we can only approve the importance he gave to inner motivations, even though he may have made an unjustified application of the principle: that we must discern God's will clearly, act with neither remorse nor doubt. This is one of the necessary requirements of sincerity and responsible action and not even a papal indult can dispense from it. What matters is intention: no authorization can make good something which is bad. All these principles advanced by Bernard are correct. What remains to be seen is whether the events to which he applied them corresponded to the way he presented them.

Quite right too is the idea developed in Letter 7 that it is more important to obey God than human beings; Adam should have refused to follow his abbot and submit to God. Each person must assume responsibility for himself, wrote Bernard, and he added: I am not to take his place. Throughout the letter he aimed at obliging Adam to examine the 'why' of his leaving: he wanted to bring him around to discovering what lay at the heart of his inner motivation and to acknowledge that he ought to have tried to discern God's will more clearly, instead of letting himself be carried away by persuasion and the example of Arnold, against his own conscience and his true free will.

Lastly we may ask whether Bernard was right to insist on the importance of charity, which should unite the members of a community and not divide them. Without any doubt, his teaching on right intention was correct, but did he himself, especially in this case, act in accord with it? Did he practice what he preached? If we go by his conscious motivations, the answer is yes: he did what he asked others to do. But over and beyond his explicit motives, which were good, were there not others, unconscious and insufficiently mature, which did not match the reasons he gave? Would this be the key to his outbursts of anger, or to the bad things he said about Arnold after his death, for having failed to get him to return? We have noticed several contradictions in what Bernard wrote. One thing he was conscious of was the necessity of justifying his way of acting when monks came from other monasteries to Clairvaux. But did he realize that his praise for Arnold in Letter 4 cannot be reconciled with the reproaches we find in the later letters? Whether or not Arnold deserved such praise or such reproach is for historians to determine, to the extent the documents allow them to do so: the psychological analysis of texts never dispenses us from consulting every available source of information. Perhaps, after all, the praise awarded to Arnold during his lifetime was merely a form of courtesy. At least, judging by

these few letters of Bernard, we cannot help but notice there
are certain contradictions which seem to have escaped him,
certain unresolved conflicts. One gets the impression that, at
least in this case, he needed to go through the therapy, the
exercise of discernment of spirits, which he sometimes so
skillfully practiced on others.

II. CHARITY AND HUMAN PASSIONS IN THE LETTER TO ROBERT

In Letter 1, addressed to his cousin Robert who had trans-
ferred from Cîteaux to Cluny, Bernard repeated several
times that, while he was attempting to bring him back, he
acted out of charity.[3] We may well believe that this was his
will. But was he moved by charity alone? Beneath his
words, can we sense unconscious needs, in particular a certain possessiveness? Did he use his passions in the service
of charity? And if he were charitable towards Robert and
Cîteaux, was he also charitable with regard to Cluny? Could
it be that Bernard—as happens to so many other people, including ourselves—was under the delusion of thinking himself guided by objective values here, whereas in fact he was
giving way to undeclared impulses? He was a born leader,
and he proved it when he brought all his brothers and one of
his uncles with him to Clairvaux. Robert was his cousin and
it was hard for him to see this member of his family resist-
ing him. He insisted at length that he felt like a father to
Robert, that he was like the mother to whom Solomon restored a child (¶ 10). In short, Bernard behaved like someone who has been frustrated and whose pride has been
wounded. It is satisfying to see that in this long letter he
gives free vent to all these very diverse and very mixed feelings.
For, little by little, towards the end of the text, we notice that his

---

3. See *Bernard de Clairvaux*, pp. 125-133; and above chapter II, 2.

main preoccupation is Robert's welfare: charity wins the day, and everything else is integrated with it.

III. SEEKING THE GLORY OF GOD AND SELF-ASSERTION

After having greatly contributed to bringing an end to the schism between Anacletus and Innocent II, Bernard took advantage of the prestige he had won in the eyes of the pope to try to persuade him to approve the nomination of one of his relatives, Geoffrey de la Roche-Vanneau, a monk of Clairvaux, as bishop of Langres in the place of the cluniac monk who had been elected to the see.[4] On this occasion Bernard wrote a series of letters which reveal in him a real aggressiveness, which we need not here describe again.[5] But let us examine Bernard's intentions. He seems as little scrupulous in the presentation of the facts as he was sure of the will of God, which, he said, he wanted to be carried out. He refused to let anyone see this will in other terms; Bernard alone is right and everyone must think the same as he. He was sure he was acting solely for the glory of God; anyone who thought otherwise was wrong. The candidate of his choice was 'the man pleasing to God'.[6] Likewise, at the end of Letter 346, concerning the election at York, he says, 'I am not speaking on my own authority but on the testimony of those who are led by the Spirit of God'. In this instance his claim to be faithful and sole representative of God's mind is all the more insistent in that he not only uses biblical reminiscences but even directly quotes in part what Christ said of himself. The first words: 'I am not speaking on my own authority...' are inspired directly by several

---

4. On the events, see Giles Constable, 'The Disputed Election at Langres in 1138', *Traditio* 13 (1957) 119-152.

5. See above chapter II, pp. 31-33.

6. Ep 164.

words of Jesus related in the Gospel according to Saint John (7:17, 8:18,38, 12:49-50), and in particular 'The words I have spoken, I have not spoken on my own authority...'. The next part of the phrase 'but on the testimony of...' repeats words which Jesus, in Saint John, often applied to himself. The end, 'who are led by the Spirit of God', is taken from a sentence in Saint Paul's letter to the Romans (8:14), which ends 'are sons of God'.[7] In cases like these Bernard seemed to insinuate that people who thought as he did had a monopoly on the Holy Spirit. There, as in many other letters, he readily identified his own friendships with the Lord's: Recommending the abbot of la Bénisson-Dieu to the archbishop of Lyons, he declared, 'All that you will do in his favor, you will do to me, or rather to Jesus Christ himself'.[8] Bernard seems to have been a very determined man, and very sure of himself; to oppose Bernard was to oppose God. Everyone was supposed to realize that Bernard's will was God's will.

IV. TOUCHINESS AND DOMINEERING TENDENCIES IN THE CLASH WITH ABELARD

How very complex were the circumstances which prepared and framed the bringing to judgement of Abelard in 1140 by what is pompously called the Council of Sens, and which in fact was a gathering of only six bishops in the presence of the king of France and a crowd of people who came mainly from the town itself, is well known. The teaching attributed to Abelard on different points of dogma and ethics formed only one of the elements in an immense complex of psychological and spiritual events, in connection with monastic, political, and ecclesiastical issues which had long

7. Ep 169.
8. Ep 173.

brought Bernard and Abelard into conflict.[9]

The arguments of a doctrinal nature were set out mainly by Bernard in a long letter to Innocent II which took the form of a treatise denouncing Abelard's errors. Before composing this letter Bernard apparently did not take the time to make a careful, personal examination of the writings of his adversary, but gave too much credit to the presentation of facts made by William of Saint Thierry who had long considered Abelard's teaching a menace to the integrity of faith. And as other elements, not at all connected with theology, also came into play, many of the reasons invoked by Bernard there and elsewhere against Abelard were simply arguments *ad hominem*, in the sense that he was attacking not only the weak spots in Abelard's personality but also addressing the sore points of the members of the roman curia to whom his letters were addressed.

Underlying the doctrinal controversy was a clash over monastic tendencies. Doubtless, Abelard in some of his writings demonstrated a reforming spirit, a sense of simplicity and austerity very akin to the cistercian program put forward by Bernard.[10] But just as he was antifeminist in theory[11] and a defender of feminine values in practice,[12] he was also in fact nearer Cluny than Cîteaux. This was not unknown to Ber-

9. The history of this conflict has been frequently studied, in particular by J. Miethke, 'Abaelards Stellung zur Kirchenreform. Eine biographische Studie', in *Francia. Forschungen zur Westeuropäischen Geschichte* 1 (1972) 158-192, with ample bibliography.

10. This is what is shown by the texts analyzed in '"Ad ipsam sophiam Christum". Le témoignage monastique d'Abélard', in *Revue d'ascétique et de mystique* 46 (1970) 165-167: 'S. Jean-Baptiste et le prophétisme monastique', and, especially by a long sermon in treatise form for the feast of Saint John Baptist, PL 178: 582-607.

11. The fact that Abelard was 'less feminist than most spiritual authors' of his times has been pointed out by R. Javelet, *Image et ressemblance au XIIe siècle* (Paris, 1967) 1: 241.

12. Cp. '"Ad ipsam sophiam Christum"' pp. 164-181: 'Moniales et diaconesses'.

nard or to the man who urged him to write against Cluny and
Abelard, William of Saint Thierry, the Benedictine with a
cistercian soul. He it was who persuaded Bernard to throw
himself into the doctrinal fray. Perhaps at first the abbot of
Clairvaux was less vexed by the whole business than his
friend, but he wanted to do him a favor and he probably did
not foresee the immense proportions the affair was to take
on. On this occasion he lets us see clearly another of his
deep tendencies, one in contrast to what he thought he
detected in Abelard. By nature Bernard was more inclined to
contemplate mystery than to scrutinize and explain it;
Abelard did not hesitate to raise new questions about matters
of faith and to seek to answer them by a method which
seemed to set more store by rational effort than by the acceptance of tradition. All this went against the grain of Bernard's innermost aspirations, for he was a man of faith and
prayer. At that time, he was enjoying a renown which
seemed to give him authority in the field of church politics
if not in theology. Thus several of the arguments he put forward were tactical rather than doctrinal. In particular he did
his utmost to put his readers on guard in advance against
Abelard and his teaching. In this way he conditioned, so to
speak, those to whom he wrote by frightening them. For example, at the beginning of a letter to Cardinal Guy he wrote:
'It is a matter of Christ; it is Christ who is concerned; truth
is at stake, Christ's tunic is being divided and the sacra-
ments of the Church are being destroyed...'. If all that had
really been true, a high church dignitary would have had
every reason to be upset, and if he should happen by chance
to be exactly informed about the doctrines being debated he
would have had trouble standing up to this sort of blackmail.
Therefore Bernard made it his business to point out the consequences of these premises: 'If you are a son of the Church,
if you do not turn away from her maternal breast, do not
leave your mother in danger, do not refuse her your shoulder

in this hour of trial'.[13]

In energetic terms Bernard went about influencing each of his correspondents by setting their formidable responsibilities before their eyes. He wrote to all the cardinals and bishops of the roman curia, 'Act in keeping with your position, in keeping with the dignity with which you are invested, according to the power you have received, so that the man who wants to rear up to heaven may be hurled into the abyss...'. That is only the beginning of a long sentence which continues in the same vein.[14] Sometimes Bernard went still further and came very near flattery, as, for example, when he wrote to the bishop of Palestrina: 'I am telling you about the anguish and the groanings of the Bride of Christ and I do so in all confidence, knowing you are a friend of the Bridegroom and that you rejoice to hear his voice. I am absolutely sure in the Lord, because I know you intimately, that you are seeking not your own interests but Christ's. And now here is Peter Abelard showing himself in his life, his discourses and his books, to be a persecutor of the catholic faith and an enemy of the cross of Christ...'.[15]

Another of Bernard's tricks in this polemic was to correlate doctrinal danger and political peril by associating Abelard and Arnold of Brescia. Arnold had criticized the wealth of the curia and attempted to stir the Romans up against the pope. Innocent II consequently opposed him from the outset. Bernard claimed that Arnold was protecting Abelard like the weapons-porter of Goliath as he went out to attack David, and he develops this comparison between these two enemies of Christ, the Church, the papacy, and truth.[16] On the basis of these considerations, Bernard assumed that Abelard would be condemned and he counted

13. Ep 334.
14. Ep 188.
15. Ep 331.
16. Ep 189.3.

him so even before the pope handed down a sentence. By the end of this same letter to Innocent II, Bernard was already treating the accused as a schismatic and a heretic and flattering the pope again. Alluding to the Anacletan schism which he had helped bring to an end, something in which he now gloried, he went on to say, 'Already on the occasion of the schism, the Lord tested you and found you worthy. But so that nothing should be missing from your crown, heresies have now sprung up. So to complete your virtues and in order that you may be found in no way inferior to those great bishops, your predecessors, dearly loved Father catch for us, these little foxes who are destroying the Lord's vineyard...'.[17]

By every possible means, making use of considerations having nothing to do with doctrine, Bernard tried to impose his own judgement on his correspondents, and on his readers, too, because he surely knew that his letters would be handed round and that some of them would one day be published, as in fact he himself was careful to ensure some years later. He probably used similar arguments to pressure the bishops who convened at Sens on the eve of the day they were to meet in council to hear and judge Abelard. But Abelard went to have an opportunity to defend himself and not for the purpose of receiving a sentence already passed on him. Not being able to plead his cause, he had recourse to Rome, a move which put the bishops in a delicate position because they, along with the king and many others, wanted France to be independent of Rome. On the other hand, the pope and the roman curia liked being appealed to because their power was highlighted. As a result of Abelard's move, Bernard had to write post-haste to as many members of the curia as possible to ensure that Abelard would be judged and condemned as a heretic even before he arrived in Rome. The arguments arising from Bernard's psychology were not the only ones in the game, but he used all his talent and his pas-

17. Ep 189.5.

sion to mix doctrinal considerations with other factors at play in the subtle game of religious politics.

This ambiguity recurs constantly in the way Bernard denounced his adversary. Sometimes he criticized his teaching on a theoretical level; sometimes he attacked his person using biblical words, letting Scripture say what he wanted to: 'Master Peter Abelard, a monk without a rule, a prelate without zeal, does not keep to the straight way and conforms to no order. He is an individual full of contradiction: inwardly he is Herod while outwardly he plays the role of John the Baptist. He is full of falseness: there is nothing of the monk in him except the name and the habit...'.[18] That should have been enough to condemn his supporters and allies. Towards the end of his letter to Cardinal Yves, we read this admonition: 'Yet he does not hesitate to say that he has supporters among the cardinals and priests of the curia. He refers to them in order to defend his past and present errors, these very men whom he ought rather to fear will judge and condemn him'. So then, just as Abelard's friends are enemies of the good of the Church, God's friends must oppose him: 'If anyone has the Spirit of God, let him remember these words of the psalm: "Do I not hate them that hate Thee, O Lord? And do I not loathe them that rise up against Thee?"'[19]

Another method Bernard used to discredit Abelard consisted in applying insulting names to him, identifying him with the most detested heretics: Arius, Pelagius, Nestorius.[20] This was of course a traditional theme and it proves nothing, but it was enough to dishonor his adversary in some not very discerning minds. It should, however, be pointed out that Bernard never attacked Abelard's past private life or his

---

18. Ep 193. Bernard alludes here, perhaps, to the fact that Abelard had presented his ideas on monasticism in the sermon on John the Baptist cited above, n.10.

19. *Ibid.*, quoting Ps 138:21.

20. Ep 331.

love affair with Heloise, which would have been an easy target for his scorn. A little later Peter Beranger, in defending Abelard, did not hesitate to take a different approach and to reproach Bernard for his youthful misdemeanors.[21] The discretion of the abbot of Clairvaux in such matters reveals a concern for dignity which does him honor.

At the same time he attacked Abelard, Bernard justified himself: If he wished to impose his own ideas, it is, he said, because he sincerely believed them better. He likened himself to David, the prophets, Saint Paul. It is as though he foresaw that he would be criticized for his intervention in this case and compared his role in it to that played by the servants of God in the Old and New Testament. He projected his own role and ideas onto Innocent II. He asked the pope to make his ideas his own, so sure was he that they were right. He tried in every way to give his action a justification valid in his own eyes and acceptable to others.

But what was he really justifying? Was it not partly, and unconsciously, his own needs, in particular his undoubted tendency to dominate others—in this case Abelard on one hand, and the pope and roman curia on the other? When he had settled on a path he thought best—whether in the monastic life, doctrine or politics—he kept to it, even though it meant being blind to other aspects of the situation. Still more, he wanted everyone to share his opinions, even at the risk of insufficiently taking into account the personality of his opponents. Consequently, he easily became dogmatic in his advice and in the judgement he passed on people and events. Such an attitude is, to some extent, courageous; it was impossible for Bernard to live in a state of conscious, willed, and accepted ambiguity, even though something of this may have remained unconsciously in his behavior. Because of the absolute nature of his character and because he sincerely believed he was in the right, he was extremely sensitive

21. *Apologeticus contra Beatum Bernardum*; PL 178:1857A-B.

to criticism coming from Abelard and his disciples and from a few members of the curia. This touchiness comes out in the letters he wrote at the time.

Later, when he published the register of his correspondence, he left out some of these letters. There may be several reasons for this: a concern to avoid repetition, to edit only the more personal letters, those he and not his secretaries had penned himself, in particular Nicolas of Montièramey whom he had trusted too much, as he was soon to discover to his great regret. But may we not also conjecture that he was sorry for having used strong words in some of his letters and therefore preferred that they be not too widely circulated? At least when he dictated or drafted them in the heat of the polemic, he demonstrated consistency and constancy. Not only his ideas but also his passions, feelings, and emotions were pressed into service. Almost as if he were afraid to come up against others, and especially against Abelard, a great dialectician, he kept strictly, even narrowly, to the schema of thought and the line of conduct he had adopted at the beginning of the conflict. A certain inflexible rigidity made him impervious to any point of view but his own and he was unmoved by contradiction. He could consider this dispute, tarred with passion on both sides, only from the standpoint of faith, and on this level he knew he was on solid ground. Did this feeling hide a certain unconscious fear for his own stability? It is not easy to say. Yet, it is clear that he intended to be faithful to himself and to what he thought God required of him: God, who alone has the right to judge what part in this conflict Abelard actually reserved to a love of truth.

Chapter VI

SAINT BERNARD AND THE FEMININE

To understand a man, especially a churchman, it is always interesting to know how he reacts to femininity. Bernard wrote several letters to women, five of them to nuns,[1] but his reactions are better seen in the long work over a period of eighteen years. Naturally, in keeping with the theme of this biblical book, there is much talk of women, especially of a young bride. The love relationship between man and woman is so frequently mentioned that Bernard could hardly avoid revealing his thoughts on the matter. The study of this very rich, well developed and varied text is a complex matter, for between the eroticism of the Song and the medieval reader was set a long biblical and patristic tradition of allegorical inspiration.[2] Was there anything left of the first sense, and did this still evoke what it was originally intended to do? Bernard had assimilated this tradition, but the fact that he knew it did not prevent him from revealing what he knew about life and love.

1. These texts have been studied in *La femme et les femmes dans l'oeuvre de Saint Bernard* (Paris, 1983) 29-38. [English translation pp 53-68] and this text revised accordingly from the French original. See also M. d'Elia Angiolillo. 'L'epistolario femminile di San Bernardo', in *Analecta s.o.c.* 15 (1959) 23-78.

2. The problems raised by the literary genre and the interpretation of the Song of Songs have been the object of numerous, sometimes divergent, studies. See, for example, L. Krinetzki, 'Die erotische Psychologie der Hohen Liedes', in *Theologische Quartalschrift* 150 (1970) 404-416, which gives a highly erotic interpretation of the Song inspired by C.G. Jung; F. Pepin, *Noces de feu. Le symbolisme nuptial du 'Cantico espiritual' de S. Jean de la Croix à la lumière du Canticum canticorum* (Paris-Tournai, 1972). In 448 very well documented pages, Pepin shows that the Song has always, since pre-christian jewish tradition, had a symbolical and spiritual significance.

A computer would surely help us—however mechanically— to discover the constants of his vocabulary and consequently of his imagination. But without recourse to it, we may well think it hardly possible for him to write some dozen sermons on the kiss and as many on the breasts of the bride and so on, without first representing what he was going to describe. Master writer that he was, he possessed the art of attracting the reader's attention from time to time by concrete details which forestalled the boredom which might result from a lofty tone too long maintained. This array of literary and psychological details are worth studying but only if we first set forth a few methodological precautions.

The difficulties are legion. The first arises from the sacred nature of the Song itself, from the twin fact that it was read in Latin and heard in an atmosphere of worship and contemplation. People were preconditioned: they knew it had a spiritual sense, and the biblical and patristic language in which the text of the words was received came between the original meaning and the interpretation spontaneously given to them in the liturgy. In our own day, our attempt to read one of the most beautiful french translations of Saint Bernard's *Sermons on the Song*[3] in a choir of monks was disappointing, almost shocking: There is nothing in it of the original depth, the richness, the religious overtones which rise, sentence by sentence, from the fabric of biblical and liturgical reminiscences to which an attentive ear would be sensitive and recognize from the original text. Any translation, even that done by authors versed in church Latin—for example, that done, and well done, by an irish Trappist[4]—is either too vague or too specific. The many harmonies that should be there are always missing; it is like a song without accompaniment. We may lawfully, therefore, in the following

3. Albert Beguin, *S. Bernard. Oeuvres mystiques* (Paris, 1953).

4. A. Luddy, *St. Bernard's Sermons on the Canticle of Canticles* (Dublin, 1920).

pages, risk giving quotations which are really paraphrases or, when the text is long, evocative summaries, rather than translations which pretend to be exact. A study of the successive translations of Saint Bernard's commentary, from those made shortly after his own day[5] up through that of Dom Antoine de Saint-Gabriel,[6] 'a seventeenth century feuillant (which Gilson preferred)'[7] and those of the nineteenth century[8] and finally those of today[9], would doubtless reveal the transformations of a language more or less marked by ancient biblical versions.[10]

The present pages will not deal with the doctrinal content of the Sermons. They will try simply to discern some of the psychological mechanisms at work as this doctrine was thought out and expressed. The collaboration of a group of psychologists has proven very valuable in this connection. Among other advantages was the fact that we were obliged to make a constant effort to be objective. But it involved the danger of projecting, from outside, problems and solutions peculiar to men of our own century onto a man who represents the culture of the past. It was important therefore to remain free in using these methods. There remains the danger that a monk may interpret a great 'erotic' and yet

5. One of these translations is preserved in a manuscript of the end of the twelfth century: see *Recueil d'études* 2 (Rome, 1966) p. 254.

6. The translation, which appeared in 1682, was re-edited the following year, according to L. Janauschek, *Bibliographia Bernardina (Vienna, 1959) nn. 1254 and 1261.*

7. *Étienne Gilson, S. Bernard. Un itinéraire du retour á Dieu* (Paris, 1964) p. 43, applied to this translation the praise Sainte-Beuve made of translations of the seventeenth and eighteenth centuries, which had 'the merit of being read by all with the pleasure and ease of an original'.

8. List of translations in Janauschek, p. 500; French translations were the most numerous.

9. A new English translation has appeared in the *Cistercian Fathers Series*, Cistercian Publications, Kalamazoo, Michigan (four volumes).

10. On the biblical translations—in particular those of the Song—used by S. Bernard, see *Recueil* 1:305-316.

'spiritual' text in the light of his own experience or lack of experience. For, in the areas of eroticism perhaps, and certainly of spirituality Bernard knew more than many of his readers. He managed to avoid talking about himself and he was careful not to impose his own images. We must be as respectful of him as he was of others.

I. SUBLIMATION: DIFFICULT OR NATURAL?

When Bernard commented, as a christian and a monk, on a poem which is really a song about human love, we may expect to find in his work—and this proves to be true—the constant presence of two sorts of data: on the one hand , the spiritual message being transmitted; and, on the other hand, the pleasure given by the text conveying the message and by the language by which it is transmitted. We have then constantly to go back and forth between text and meaning, and Bernard never hides the fact that this is not always easy, and presents obstacles to be overcome.

He said so clearly in the first sermon:

> This is a pleasant discourse which begins with a kiss! The smiling face of this part of Scripture readily captivates us and moves us to read on. What a delight it is to seek its hidden meaning, even though this may be difficult! And we are not wearied by the difficulty of the search because the sweetness of the language charms us.... Here then is a text skillfully composed by the Holy Spirit in such a way that it is difficult to understand and yet pleasant to interpret (1.5; SBOp 1:5,12-18).[11]

11. In the references henceforth given in the text, the first figure indicates the sermon, the next the paragraph; then in roman numerals comes the volume, next the page and the line, or lines, in the critical

And a little further on he says: 'Here Solomon has expressed the mysteries of sacred and eternal love in pleasant but figurative language' (1.8;SBOp 1:6,13-16). Over and beyond the images, but by their intermediary, then, we must always reach out towards the mystery, and if these images are delightful agree to enjoy them for the moment.

This duality in the opposing facts, and consequently in the reactions of both reader and interpreter, recurs as a constant theme:

> We could not find sweeter names to express the mutual feelings of the Word and the soul than that of bride and bridegroom. Between them everything is held in common, nothing belongs to one alone, there is no division: For the two there is only one single heritage, one table, one house, one bed, and, even more, one flesh. Indeed, in view of all this, a man shall leave his father and his mother and be joined with his spouse and they two shall become one flesh.

All that is intended to evoke 'sacred love', 'a very chaste spouse who cannot hide the flame consuming her'. In these texts of Bernard we always find conciliation between real, true love and a no less genuine chastity: 'she loves, but chastely; she loves, but holily; she loves, but ardently...' (7.2-3;SBOp 1:31,23-32,18).

Bernard frequently mentions the difficulty we have in shifting from one register to another. In connection with the kiss of the lips he writes: 'Listen more carefully to what is to be savored more sweetly, tasted more rarely, and understood less easily' (8.1;I:36,14-15). Is this difficulty merely a

---

edition, *Sancti Bernardi Opera* 1 (Rome, 1957) [Sermons 1-35], 2 (Rome, 1958) [Sermons 36-86].

literary theme, a way of saying that there is a mystical sense
more lofty than what the words lead us to think? Or is it really a psychological difficulty which Bernard confesses he
found it hard to overcome, as though the pleasure of the language of human love tempted him to linger over it unduly?
We cannot say for sure. Sometimes he gives the impression
that he took a certain pleasure in describing the bride or the
relations she has with the bridegroom. As soon as he realized this, he set in motion a mechanism of sublimation and
moved up from concrete facts to symbols. He makes excuses, justifies himself, says it was necessary to be specific
about the literary sense, and then soars up to the heights of
mystical theology. From the first phase of this spontaneous
process he was realistic without being vulgar. And he never
waited until he got to lofty considerations to turn everything
into poetry and music by the quality of his comparisons and
the rhythm of his sentences. It is beauty which transforms
everything, even before spiritual intention gives human love
its full value, whereby everything having to do with sense,
experience far from being denied, is used and integrated into
a richer experience transcending it.

For example, Bernard was aware of the psychology of
married couples and especially their tendency to jealousy:

> 'Joseph had been given power over all his egyp-
> tian master's possessions, but he knew that the
> wife of his master was an exception: Therefore he
> refused to approach her... He knew that a wife is
> the glory of her husband, and he found it iniq-
> uitous to strike a blow at the glory of the man who
> had raised him to glory. With the wisdom and the
> prudence of a man of God, he realized that a hus-
> band is always jealous of his wife, as of his own
> glory, and that he intended to keep her for himself
> and not give her to another. Joseph refused to lay
> hands on something which had not been entrusted

to him' (13.4;1:70,27-71,6).

And only after having discreetly but specifically mentioned this psychological fact did Bernard go on to speak at length about the spiritual theme of God's jealously for the man whom he has called to his service.

We could pick out allusions throughout these sermons to indicate Bernard's personal psychology. It is, for example, evident that the bride's breasts evoked motherhood. But that he should apply this to prelates implies a deliberate choice on his part: 'Learn to be mothers for your subjects, not dominators...You will be mothers when you caress, fathers when you correct...'. And the symbolism of swelling breasts is developed so realistically and so precisely that it really works only in Latin (23.2;1:140,1-5). Why did Bernard take pleasure in such images? Was it because of their specifically feminine, or more precisely maternal, nature? Do we have any clues that he had possessive tendencies? These are so many questions which we may only ask with prudence and to which we can only try to give wary answers.

A little later in the same sermon, allusions to the bed-chamber, to the various liberties the king allows the queen, the concubines, and other young women, to the pleasant and secret presence of the bridegroom there where he lies down and rests at midday may say more to one reader than another or to Bernard himself. What naïve repressions can be covered up by the erotic interpretation given by certain commentators! The final part of sermon 23, on the verse 'The king had led me to his bed-chamber', is a masterpiece of suggestive poetry. Everything may have a double meaning, but the reader who took pleasure in it would surely be more responsible than the author. This warning against the abuse of double meanings could be backed up by other examples.

One thing is sure: Bernard knew how to describe a pretty girl. 'A black pupil never spoils the beauty of an eye...and black hair gives further charm to the beauty of a fair face...'

(25.3;1:164,15-17). What church writer or preacher today would dare venture on to such ground? But in an era that was not 'eroticized', where words were words, where images conjure up nothing but themselves, where nothing deviated from its first meaning or was exploited for indefensible ends, Bernard could guilelessly use such language. Further on yet, taking care to warn us that we must not 'think about them in a carnal way', he speaks delicately about the bride's cheeks, her skin, her complexion (40.1;SBOp 2:24,15-19), her neck, pretty enough, well formed not to need ornaments (41.1;2:28,11-18), her face gently blushing with modesty (42.1;2:33,16). We may suppose that had he come to the final chapter of the Song, where the bride's body is admired in some detail, he would have written with the same tact. And the very fact that he never felt the need to comment on this chapter is proof enough that he was not obsessed by these details.

Yet, he was a man of flesh and blood and a poet sensitive to beauty. He did not refuse to use his imagination in order to make his message more convincing, more attractive and, I might dare say, more enticing. The author of the Song says of the bridegroom 'Behold he comes leaping on the mountains, skipping over the hills. And the psalms likened him to a giant.' Bernard goes on to say 'Let us depict (*pingemus*) a tall man, a giant who has fallen in love with a poor little woman, and she is away. He hurries to the embrace he desires. He leaps over the mountains and the hills which rise so high above the ground and the plains that sometimes their summits pierce the clouds. But it does not do for us to give way to these sense representations in connection with this spiritual Song, especially we who read in the Gospel 'God is spirit and those who worship him must worship him in spirit' (53.3;2:97,22-98,1).

Thus, as we see, there are always two levels: the sense level, which is part of our being as God created us; and the level of the Holy Spirit, who has been spread abroad in our hearts. Bernard the writer was never unaware of either. He knew that there is an order, a hierarchy between them. He does not seem to have found it difficult—even though he sometimes said it was not easy—to integrate the first with the second. Are we in this connection to speak of sublimation? We may, provided we do not give this word a precise technical sense. If there was any sublimation it seems very likely that it went on beforehand, once and for all. It was not the result of an effort which had to be renewed each time a new image or an expression liable to an erotic meaning cropped up. There are symbols which can rouse sexual echoes but which an author—and the readers he had in mind—can sufficiently 'sublimate', and use without any complexes. There is not even any need to make a conscious passage from the image to the reality signified. We have there a fact which could be illustrated by a long tradition of commentators of the Song of Songs and which everything in Bernard's case seems to confirm. Did he not, at the beginning of the first sermon warn us that this book of the Bible is not to be put into everyone's hands and that he supposes that he is dealing with a reader who had come to the maturity of adulthood?

In order to test this conjecture more closely, let us now examine two groups of sermons, those at the beginning and at the end of the commentary which deal specially with two revealing symbols.

II. THE KISS: SYMBOLISM AND REALITY

1. *The texts*. In the first nine sermons Bernard speaks of the kiss in commenting on the first verse of the Song, 'Let him kiss me with the kiss of his lips'. This is a theme on which

he frequently preached, as other texts attested.[12] Here, however, we have a long, uniform, and specific development. From a psychological point of view, the reason it is worth studying rather than the others, is that this is probably the text in which Bernard expressed most clearly his thought on one of the acts expressive of human love. Having commented on only the first two chapters of the Song, he did not have to explain other manifestations of love mentioned later on.

In these first long nine sermons, taking up some fifty pages, he builds, in the spiritual interpretation of the first verse, a clever and subtle scale rising, so to speak, from the humility of 'Certainly not on the lips!' to the sublimeness— not too strong a word, for here 'lips' should be written with a capital—the sublimeness of the Lip, divine the Kiss exchanged between the Father and the Son (7.7-8). Bernard and his readers arrive at this by going from a kiss bestowed on the feet, on the hands, even on the mouth, whereas at first this was excluded. But the ascent is irresistible: we are carried up even higher, from symbol to symbol. Yet it is clear that underlying all this symbolism is the plain kiss mentioned in the verse being commented on: the kiss exchange on the lips, two lovers.

The allusions to the kiss are many. Some are sometimes clear enough to be real descriptions. It is a 'contact of the lips' which sometimes takes the place of union of spirits (2.2;1:9,13-14), so not every kiss is necessarily a proof of love. It may be simply an occasion of pleasure. There is a difference between the pressing of two mouths and the embrace of two hearts really in love (2.4;1:10,13). 'When we say to one another "kiss me" or "Give me a kiss" no one ever thinks of adding "with your lips" or "a kiss of your lips". Why, if not that when we get ready to kiss we bring

12. *De diversis*, 87 and 89; SBOp 6/1 (Rome, 1970) 329 and 335; *Sent* 1.8, and 2.164; SBOp 6/2 (Rome, 1972) 9 and 55.

our mouths together and there is no need to name them'(4.1;1:18,20-23).

> She who loves asks a kiss and nothing else.... She lives on love and is utterly incapable of hiding the flame consuming her. And that is why she lets slip such an opening to her discourse: at the very moment when she is going to ask something great of this person, she does not prepare her speech. She does not wrap her request up in roundabout phrases, as we usually do. She makes no preamble, she does not try to ingratiate, but suddenly blurting it out, she lets the abundance of her heart pour out and in naked, shameless language says: 'Let him kiss me with a kiss of his lips!' (7.3;1:32,6-14). What friendly and familiar conversation! These are kisses: she asks what she longs for. She does not speak the name of the man she loves, for she never doubts that they know him, these people with whom she has so often spoken of him. She does not say: 'Let so and so kiss me'; but only 'Let him kiss me!' (7.8.p.35,21-25).

Do we not have here the refinements of the language of courtly love?

A little further on, in the last of the nine sermons which deal with the kiss, we find a dialogue of jealous love which could be profane and read in a novel. The friends of the bridegroom come to speak to the betrothed, or more exactly to the bride, for there is now a legitimate marriage to which she has been unfaithful by chasing after other lovers. It begins as if it were a jealousy scene and ends with a scene of pardoned infidelity. The friends of the bridegroom find the bride in a bad mood: 'What happened to you? Didn't you run after other lovers who failed to please you, so that now you are forced to come back to your first husband?'. And they batter her with questions to which she answers only yes or no until her love bursts out: she blurts out the words 'I love', 'I desire', and she intones a hymn to love: 'I am carried away by my desire and not by reason... Modesty has its rights, but love is stronger...'. Once more she begs for a kiss on the lips (9.1-2;1:42-43).

The application of this symbolism to the forgiveness of sins and the desire for God comes only later. Obviously Bernard took pleasure using the theme of the kiss to write first a beautiful page about love. He even felt obliged to excuse himself for having dwelt at such length on this kiss and to justify himself: 'But I have spent enough time on this kiss, even though, I must confess, I have not yet said anything worthy of it. But since, after all, we learn about it better by receiving than by talking about it, let us go on to something else' (9.3;1:44,11-13). And he began a second group of sermons, dealing with the bride's breasts. There is yet one more realistic allusion to the kiss: 'So effective is this holy kiss that she no more than received it before she conceives and her breasts swell with milk' (9.6;46,20-22).

2. *Bernard's psychology*. Among the various things these first nine sermons let us see, we can distinguish Bernard's reaction to the feminine and the idea he had of love-making.

Woman is represented here first of all by the bride of the Song. She is mentioned more often than the betrothed, and Bernard represents her as speaking more often. It is true that the verse of the Song being commented on is put into her mouth in the text, so we cannot draw any conclusions concerning Bernard.[13] Also, in sermon six there is a brief allusion to the 'legs of the Bridegroom which are like pillars of

13. P. Trille, 'The Bible and Women's Liberation', in *Theology Digest* 22 (1974) 35, demonstrates the preeminent feminine element of the Canticle's structure and composition, from the kiss the Bride asks for at the outset to the description given of her at the end.

marble on golden bases' (6.7;1:29,18-20): these images come from chapter five of the Song. Examples drawn from women seem to be more numerous than those suggested by men: we have the Ethiopian girl— of whom Bernard also spoke elsewhere[14]— who though black became white (3.2;1:15,4), Magdalen kissing the Lord's feet (3.2;1:15,14-18); and the captive daughter of Zion who, when freed, shook off the dust which covered her (3.2;1:15,19-20). Magdalen, whose sins were forgiven her, is mentioned once again (6.4;1:28,4); she comes on the scenes later, as well (7.8;1:35,25). We do find David mentioned, it is true, and other repentant sinful men. But a rough calculation would seem to show a preference for female examples among all the possibilities offered by the Bible. And there is a feminine element in virtue of which every christian can see himself as a 'daughter of the Father, a bride or sister of the Son' (8.9,1:41,20), a comparison built on a series of texts taken from both Old and New Testaments.

What can we conjecture from these sermons about the idea Bernard had of the love relationship between a man and a woman? In comparison with everything he says about the other things, he does not give much room to love-making. He was not obsessed with it, he mentioned it enough for us to know that he was informed on the subject. As to sexual activity, to the extent that it becomes genital, he was certainly not ignorant. Sometimes throughout his work and in these nine sermons, he speaks clearly of temptations and sins of the 'flesh', and not only in the sense this word gener-

---

14. *Parable* 6 on the *Ethiopian married to the king's son*, SBOp 6/2:286-295; it has parallels in the *Sentences* of Bernard, as pointed out by H. Rochais, 'Enquête sur les Sermons divers de S. Bernard', in *Analecta S.O.C.* 18 (1962) 42-43. In pre-christian and christian antiquity, the Ethiopians, considered very black, were the symbol of all blacks, as has been shown by Frank M. Snowden, Jr, *Blacks in Antiquity* (Cambridge, Mass, 1971) 2-4. On the theme of blackness in the Song and its commentators, see his pp. 198-201.

ally has in Saint Paul, where it means the human condition
without grace or opposed to grace, but in the more precise
sense that it sometimes has both in Saint Paul and in tradition, and which it too often has in modern times, linked with
sexuality. Bernard supposed that fleshly temptations are
overcome and left behind—which implies that people experience them as a normal thing. He talks about them calmly,
without stressing them or complicating them, as one of the
facts of life for everyone, including himself. He even speaks
of himself in this regard, not without some literary exaggeration, as if he wanted to put others at ease and not seem
to overwhelm them.[15]

In these nine sermons, beginning in the very first one, he
alludes to the 'daily experience' of his monks who are supposed to be listening to him. This experience has brought
them out of misery and mud—forceful images taken from the
Bible (1.9;1:6,22-24). He mentions the 'daily combats which
are never lacking to those who wish to live generously in
Christ, combats arising from the world, the flesh, and the
devil', 'temptation overcome, vice controlled, one or other
old, inveterate habit cured' (1.9;1:7,5-11). Later on we come
across 'the soul burdened with its sins, still given up to the
passions of the flesh and unable to savor the delights of the
spirit' (3.1;1:14,17-18). It is never said that all this applies
to sexual things; but this is not excluded. The general impression is one of good spiritual health which has been
acquired—or rather won—and kept at the cost of some effort.

A keen sense of sin is kept alive in every christian by the
memory of past sins and the possibility of relapsing into
them (3.3;1:15,27-16,5). The result is a kind of shame
(*verecundia*) which is the opposite to shamelessness: a guil-
tiness which has nothing unhealthy about it because it is not

15. 'S. Bernard et l'expèrience chrètienne', in *Aspects du monachisme
hier et aujourd'hui* (Paris, 1968) 261-277; English translation, *Aspects of
Monasticism* (Kalamazoo, 1978) 251-266.

a pathological regret about the past, but humility in the presence of God, trust in the help he continues to give (3.3-4;1:16,5-16). Everyone knows that this is the common condition of humankind and there is no false modesty in talking about it.

In the ninth sermon we read an allusion to a difficult but possible chastity. It is mentioned, it is true, in scriptural terms which might also mean something other than chastity: 'And now, by his grace, I have for long years been living carefully in chastity and temperance. I give myself to reading and I resist vice, I pray frequently, am on my guard against temptation, and think with bitterness over my soul's past' (9.2;1:43,16-18).

In short, when we try to find in these sermons of Bernard allusions of this kind and then put them together and interpret them, we get the impression that where as courtly literature is erotic, varying in elegance and probably for the use of a minority, monastic literature is chaste. We do find *eros* in it as something known and acknowledged, something conscious and on the surface in these texts. But it is not exploited: there is no process of 'erotization'. Like Peter Damian— though with the nuances unique to each personality— Bernard of Clairvaux appears as a bachelor religious, someone who has chosen to live in this state, sensitive to what is feminine yet at peace.[16] He was a happy monk.

III. THE DIALOGUE OF LOVE

Vox dilecti mei. 'I hear the voice of my beloved'. In the final twenty-five sermons, the bride and the bridegroom are going to come together; or at least they think they are. The

---

16. On the subject of Peter Damian, see texts cited in 'S. Pierre Damien et les femmes', *Studia monastica* 15 (1973) 43-55.

betrothed hears the voice of her beloved; then, little by little, she sees him coming. Each phase of their meeting could be studied: it consists of search, approach, exchanged glances, new separations. Each lover yearns for the other, as in some eastern dance, slow-slow, quick-quick, languishingly slow. A ballet like this is noticed especially at the beginning of the sermons, where Bernard explains the literal sense of each verse before commenting on it at another level. From his pen, as in the text of the Song, we suspect real play between the lovers, with insinuations, expectations, explosions, surprises, suspense. There is no sudden possession but a long, slow mutual approach: successive visits, conversations begun, interrupted, and taken up again. Let us now look at a few explicit texts on these love plays.

1. *The play.* First we have the beginning of sermon sixty-two, where play vocabulary is used. 'Arise my beloved, my loved one, my bride, come!' The bridegroom betrays the intensity of his love by repeating words of love, for repetition is expressive of affection. He loves and goes on saying words of love. He calls her his dove, as though he were caressing her. He says that she is his, and insists that she is his alone. What she once incessantly asked for, he now asks in his turn; he wants to see her and talk with her. He behaves like a fiancé; but being bashful, he wants to avoid any public show, and decides to enjoy her charms in a secret place, in the cleft of the rock, the hollow places in the wall. 'Let us imagine then that he says to her: *Puta ergo sic dicere sponsum.*' Here we see the part played by imagination. Bernard adds something to the text, he develops first and foremost, its literal meaning.

> Let us imagine then that he says to her: 'Do not fear my darling, as if the work in the vineyard to which I am inviting you were going to hinder or interrupt our love affair (*negotium amoris*). To the

contrary, it will be useful to what both of us desire. For the vineyards have walls and hidden recesses, just what bashful people need.' Such is the play of the letter: *hic litteralis lusus*. Why not call it play? Where is the seriousness in this text? The words are not even worth listening to if the Holy Spirit does not help, from within, the feebleness of our understanding. Let us not stay outside, on the surface, lest we seem—which God forbid!— to be describing the iniquities of licentious loves. To this discourse on love lend chaste ears, and when you think of the lovers, do not think of a man and a woman, but the Word and the soul, Christ and the Church...(61.2;SBOp 2:148-149).

What ease and what art Bernard has in all this for passing from the language of love to that of charity! In his writings there are not many texts like this: the development, the *amplificatio*, of the literal sense by the imagination is rarely pushed as far as it is in this passage. More often we find only allusions to games human love plays. Did Bernard want to show that he could have said more? He was infinitely more interested in the spiritual than in the literal meaning, though he did not reject this. Once again we point out that Bernard was not in a state of repression, or inhibition; he merely controlled himself. He could have gone further into erotic imagination. He proved it. But he very soon came to a stop on this path, which did not interest him.

2. *Boiling love.* Another fairly developed passage occurs in sermon 67:

'My beloved is mine and I am his'...We know very well of whom the bride is speaking, but we do not know to whom. In fact, he is no longer there and she has to call him back saying, 'Return

my beloved'. We are led to suppose that, having
spoken, he withdrew; but she has stayed there and
gone on talking about the person who, for her, is
never absent...She talks about him, but to whom?
To her companions? I think instead that she is talking to herself and no one else, especially as her
sentence is disconnected, with no continuity, insuf-
ficient to let anyone who hears her talking to herself understand what she is talking about: 'My beloved is mine and I am his'. Nothing else? The
words hover; more exactly, they fail. The hearer is
left in suspense; he is not enlightened, but he is
stimulated' (67.1-2; 2:188-189).

For more than a page Bernard continues this description in
terms of mad love, with its violence, its sighs, and its appeals, its expressions now of joy now of sorrow, terms
which remind us of the language of precious love in seventeenth century France.. Indeed, there is only one language of
love, whether human or mystical or— why not?— both
together: 'So a burning and vehement love, especially divine
love, cannot contain itself. It pays no attention to either the
order of words, or the rules of grammar, or even to the num-
bers of words; it boils over. Sometimes it has need neither of
words nor sounds: it merely sighs. Thus the bride, aflame
with a holy love of unbelievable intensity, lets something of
the ardor she is enduring burst out. Everything swells up in
her mouth under love's impulse; she does not speak, she
cries out (67.3;190,14-22). The words Bernard used in latin
are the biblical *eructatio* and *ructus*, which are hard to translate genteelly.

It was normal, then, and easy for a man like Bernard, or
Richard Rolle, or John of the Cross, to move from the language of love to that of charity, from the dialogue between a
man and a woman to that between Christ and the Church.
How very different all this is from the erotic language of

courtly literature! It is an erotic, yet mystic, language; that
is, it is applied to mystery. Should we still call it erotic? The
temptation is to apply to it the greek word for charity and
call it 'agapic' love. Everything Bernard says about this
overflowing and unruly *ructus*, in lines of untranslatable
beauty (67.4;190-191), leaves us in no doubt of his ability to
speak about purely fleshly love had he wished to do so. But
he passed imperceptibly to a uniquely religious language.
The Bible itself provided him with the expression of these
two languages and the possibility of mingling them: the language of the Song and of Saint Paul, the language of loving
desire and prophetic desire, the desire the prophets and Bernard shared; and which is shared by those in the Church who
read both the prophets and Bernard.

We cannot savor this vocabulary, still less the language,
the latinity steeped in the Vulgate and the liturgy, unless we
take into consideration the fabric of biblical reminiscences
which make up its style. This is true of every page Saint
Bernard wrote, and far more so when reminiscences of love
come into play. The words of one love evoke, that is, call,
recall, those of another; words of love call up words of
charity; words of eros bring to the mind words of agapè. In
sermon 67, devoted to the cry of the bride, we see to what
extent the vocabulary of passionate search, in the mouth of a
betrothed, is wonderfully applicable to the experience of
faith, hope, and charity.

3. *Crescendo*. Throughout the following sermons we enjoy a
sort of crescendo of symbolism more than of realism. At the
beginning of sermon 73, for example, we have a short hymn
to 'intemperate love', which has 'gone out of its senses', the
love which, 'doing away with propriety and measure, overcoming the sense of shame, *ignoring* any deliberation,
neglecting all modesty, provokes real disorder' (73.1;
2:223,21-25). Immediately Bernard soars to the heights: 'All
this is the letter. But as for me (*ego vero*), it is quite another

matter...' (73.1-2;234,3-5). The tone is the same at the beginning of the following sermon, on the same words of the bride: 'Return, my beloved'. This time separated love is presented as being the most intense, for desire is a form of presence:

> Return: this is an untimely calling back, the proof is great, single, shared love. Who are these people who entertain charity this way, who do not weary of this love affair (*amatorium negotium*) one of whom pursues the other, who, in turn, kindles such unsatisfied love? (74.1;239,25-241,1).

Here the passage to the spiritual level is made even more quickly and in this context of mad love we find the magnificent description— I am tempted to say the magnificent music—of the visits of the Word-Bridegroom which makes this sermon one of the most important in the entire work.[17]

At the beginning of the next sermon (75) we have a detailed and exact description of the fiancée, madly in love, running all over town looking for her beloved. Here too, the literal sense is not passed over in silence; the *negotium amoris* is very realistically present. And everything could stay at that level 'if this were a matter of fleshly and shameful loves, as the surface of the letter seems to suggest. If they want such things to happen to them, that is their business, it does not interest me...' (75.1-2;2:247-248,8). A group of sermons is now devoted to the theme of the bride's quest for her lover, which is the symbol of the desire for God. The ardent crescendo leads, at the beginning of sermon 79, to a new hymn to love which could be applied to human love as well as to love for God: 'Have you seen him whom my soul loves?' O fiery, vehement, violent, impetuous love,

17. This sermon 74 is discussed from a stylistic point of view, in *Recueil d'études* 3 (Rome, 1969) 205-208.

unable to think of anything but yourself, bored with everything not yourself, contemptuous of all, satisfied with yourself! You bring disorder into everything, taking no account
of custom, ignoring moderation.' (79.1;272,5-8). On this
breathless tone of irrepressible fervor, Bernard moves imperceptibly from one love to the other. The dialogue between a man and a woman goes on; in this sense it is sexual
because she and he are both sexual. But it is not sexual in
the sense that sexual images are totally lacking, which was
not the case in the earlier sermons on the kiss.

Bernard's life was drawing to a close and his great work
was nearing completion. In sermon 83, one of the last four,
we see once again the similarity of the language used 'in
marriage which is holy and spiritual' and in human marriage
(83.3;299-300). Does this not suppose an optimistic confidence in the 'spiritual' nature of both? It is easy to understand how Bernard defended marriage against the rhineland
heretics, in sermon 66, which we should go into more
deeply. And it is easy to see, too, how he moved so easily
from the 'two in one flesh' of Genesis to Saint Paul's 'one
spirit with God'.

The three last sermons comment the words of the bride,
'In my bed at night I sought him whom my soul loves'. Entire pages are devoted to the bed, but without a single allusion to what goes on there. More important than the bed is
the love between bride and bridegroom, and between man
and God. The bed is only a symbol of the search for God. At
the end of sermon 85, Bernard affirms that love is greater
than fertility , that love between married people is greater
than affection for children (85.13;316,3-8). Several times
the word *amplexus*— loving embrace— recurs. This is not
merely the kiss, but the embrace, the total union of two
bodies, two beings. We could say that the distance covered
since the first nine sermons has brought us from *osculum* to
amplexus, from the kiss to the embrace. But, contrary to
what we might expect, the symbolism becomes less and less

precise, more and more spiritual; the physical activity is less and less important. Does this mean that Bernard went through an evolution, or is it just an effect of art? The whole of sermon 85 is the climax of the work: it is one of the longest and it is the one with the most elevated tone. Sermon 86, left unfinished, is looked upon as being a moralizing appendix on the virtue of modesty, or self-effacement, *verecundia* in the sense of humility, lack of ostentation. Yet again, there is a double meaning, since it also refers to the modesty with which the bride, throughout the nights, seeks her husband in bed. There is much talk of *secretum*, privacy. In these final pages Bernard excelled at manipulating double meanings: bed, night, darkness; everything suggests both intimacy and mystery, and comes together in light, the light proclaimed by Saint Paul when he says 'Walk as children of light' (86;2:317-320).

4. *Marriage and love.* In all these texts, love, not marriage, was the subject of discourse. But there is one sermon, sermon 66, which is different. This is one of the sermons Bernard wrote to refute the rhineland 'heretics' who, like others, have had the label 'cathars' pinned on them. They condemned weddings and what they called chastity was nothing but moral licence and free union. Against them Bernard defended the legitimacy of marriage: outside marriage there is sin unless there is voluntary continence. Beyond these two solutions there is only sensuality and immorality. Banish marriage and you let in impurity and corruption. From this perspective, is marriage an act of love and its condition? Or is it not instead a social condition, a guarantee of moral order in the area of sexuality, and a sacrament of the Church? Is there love in this case? It would not seem so. Continence is a rare gift among humans; so marriage, even a second or a third marriage in the event of widowhood, is to be advised to avoid disorder in persons and in society. (66.3-5;179-182).

All this makes us think a little of courtly literature, where discourse on love and discourse on marriage are different, where marriage and love do not coincide. Here, of course, love is not excluded. We may even think that it is supposed by all that is said elsewhere about the relations between bride and bridegroom. But except in sermon 66, there is never any mention of the social or sacramental category of marriage. Hence the difficulty of knowing each time whether *sponsus* and *sponsa* mean two lovers or the fiancé and the fiancée, or again bride and bridegroom. But in every instance love is being dealt with, and there are never any details as to how it is lived comparable to those in the sermons on the kiss. What counted for Bernard was love; all the rest was merely symbol. Bernard wrote poetry and did not go into psychological—still less physiological—descriptions.

When he used the language of love, as when he suggested the kiss, Bernard always had recourse to two orders, two levels: realism and symbolism. By the limited length of its developments and the lesser importance and value it is given, realism is always subordinated to symbolism. Yet it is neither denied nor forgotten. But the realism of human love and the symbols used to speak about it were only there to recall quite another reality: the love which Bernard knew to be charity.

IV. CONCLUSION. 'MY SECRET IS MINE'

The information which we have just presented does not pretend to be definitive. And probably no one will ever say the last word about this mystery. But at least it results from the application of a double method which guarantees the right to propose it.

The first part of our research depended on the textual and literary criticism of the *Sermons on the Song of Songs*: the

manuscript tradition, the history of the redaction, the iden-
tification of sources, an examination of the processes of
composition and expression.[18] The analysis of the theological content has generally been left to other authorities.[19]

Then the text was studied in collaboration with a team of
psychologists. They drew my attention to many details, to
images and psychic dynamisms, details of vocabulary and
style such as possible 'double meanings'—for all of which I
am grateful. I had several times read these *Sermons* in the
manuscripts, and then in the proofs, and finally in the
printed text without ever having noticed these clues to Bernard's depth psychology; I was probably occupied solely
with variants, typographical errors, or ideas. During this
fresh reading I was surprised to discover in Bernard's
masterpiece so many erotic elements which had escaped my
notice.

A few months later, I reread the *Sermons on the Song* and
found nothing of what I had for an instant thought I had
found there. It is the result of this last reading which I have
set down in these pages. It was then that I came across the
words T.R. Henn uses in his beautiful book, *The Bible as
Literature*, to describe the Song. They apply to Bernard's
commentary, and I would like to quote them here by way of
conclusion:

> There are not many great love-poems in English
> that are direct and simple, built without shame on
> the delighted senses of bride and bridegroom.
> Much western poetry is concerned with the di-

18. These works are in the second part of *Recueil d'études* 1:173-351:
'Recherches sur les Sermons sur les Cantiques'; and in *Recueil* 3 (Rome,
1969) 145-162 and *passim*.

19. The best study by far is Emero Stiegman, *The Language of
Asceticism in St Bernard of Clairvaux's 'Sermones super Cantica
canticorum'*, Dissertation, Fordham University, New York, 1973
(University Microfilms, Ann Arbor, Michigan).

vided soul of the lover, with despair, frustration, rejection or loss. A whole convention is founded on unsatisfied desire. Often it is turned inward in some form of agonized self-analysis. Here the poetry is pure, uninhibited, sensuous without trace of sensuality or lust. In these respects, as in the minutely-perceived freshness of nature, it has (as many commentators have noted) a delicate, almost feminine quality.[20]

Beyond any doubt, anyone wanting to perceive something of Bernard's attitude to the feminine must first consult his commentary on the Song of Songs. Do we not find there that Bernard reveals his genuine monastic aspiration, in that knowing—by experience, by reading, or otherwise—the plays of human love, he found greater joy in the obscure encounter with his God? But let us not nurture the illusion that we shall be able to draw his secret out of him. 'My secret is mine, my secret is mine', repeated Isaiah in a phrase Bernard applied to the bride.[21] And, indeed, this secret belongs to him alone, and to God.

20. T.R. Henn, *The Bible as Literature* (Oxford, 1970) 87-88.
21. Is 24:16, applied to the bride in Sermon 23.9; 1:144-145.

Chapter VII

PSYCHOLOGY AND HOLINESS

I. HUMILITY A CONDITION OF ACTION

Having pointed out a number of somewhat negative factors, we should not forget to mention the positive ones. In this connection one or two preliminary remarks need to be made. First, if we consider Bernard only in the light of his relations with the people who opposed him, we run the risk of neglecting the ties he had with his friends, with all those whom he had no reason to come up against, and with the many people whom he tried to help or to whom he simply wanted to give pleasure. In his 'lettres de humanité', containing personal confidences or giving spiritual advice, we see quite another, and very endearing, aspect which has not always been given enough attention by those historians who study mainly events.[1]

Then, too, it is very difficult to analyze attitudes in which psychological factors are forever being tangled up with considerations of a supernatural order. Everything hangs together and yet we are obliged to separate out certain details simply because we cannot talk about everything at once. But we must at least bear in mind the unity in which all these different states of soul come together. All we can do here is propose a series of 'approaches'. A certain amount of repetition is probably inevitable in this sort of research, but it will at least bring out a few more salient facts. What we have to

1. *S. Bernard. Lettres choisies*, a selection of these 'letters of humanity', translated into french by E. de Solms (Namur, 1962).

say in the following pages needs to be delicately nuanced and at each step we shall have to stop and wonder what Bernard himself would think. Some interpretation is unavoidable, but it is the only path to progress in our knowledge in this field: the important thing is that this knowledge is always based on the texts themselves.

Here again, as elsewhere, we have to set great store by the Prologues, not so much from the point of view of their conformity with literary tradition,[2] or of the psycho-dynamic mechanisms we guess are at play,[3] but in their connection with the intentions which Bernard mentions. It is not impossible that they reveal a spiritual journey and, certainly, we shall find in them what might be called Bernard's ongoing self-therapy. Having taken all these precautions, we may consider the interior life of the abbot of Clairvaux as one marked by a very conscious dialectic between humility and charity. Humility made him aware of his limitations and is the touch-stone of the purity of his intentions. Charity urged him to act in order to serve.

1. *Awareness of limitations.* At the outset of his literary career, in his first work, devoted to *The Steps of Humility and Pride*, Bernard gave a definition of humility: it is 'the virtue by which man, knowing himself as he really is, becomes lowly in his own eyes'. Did he see himself line up to this definition, and if so, how? As we read through many of his texts and especially his Prologues, he seems to us always to have been faced with a grave dilemma: whether to take action in the way he was asked to do—especially by writing— in which case he foresaw that he would attract 'glory', or to refuse to act because he knew full well that he would be criticized if the result did not come up to expectations. Was he conditioned by this or did he stay free? He made up his

2. *Recueil d'études sur S. Bernard* 3 (Rome, 1968) 13-32.
3. See above, chapter II, pp. 38-41.

mind, but only after having clearly envisaged two eventualities: to speak, and thus to lack humility; to remain silent, and thus to fail to render service. His capacity for seeing himself as he was, with his talents and his limitations, and for judging himself with the kind of humor which consists in standing back from self led him to beg for prayers that he might avoid both pitfalls, being neither puffed up with pride if he reaped 'glory' nor depressed and discouraged if his lot were 'shame'.[4] The very force of the words he used betrays both the keenness of the tension he observed in himself and the clearsightedness with which he looked it in the face.

One way of overcoming this antimony is to submit to another man's judgement. This Bernard willingly did, as we see in his Prologue to the treatise *On Grace and Free Choice*.[5] This amounted to acknowledging that he did not know everything, that others were more competent than he and had every right to criticize him. Would we find in Abelard, for example, the same concern to reveal self to others as one really is and to accept correction? In the Prologue of his lenten sermons on Psalm 90, and throughout the work, he speaks of temptation as a trial he suffered just like the monks he was addressing.[6] He refused to play the perfect man free from doubts and hesitations.[7] Yet in 1139, the year he wrote these sermons,[8] he had become a churchman whose effectiveness had been manifested by the part he played in ending the Anacletan schism and soon afterwards he was to oppose Abelard with great self-assurance. He knew that he was highly thought of by many. Surely it took courage to

---

4. SBOp 3:16.

5. *Ibid.*, p. 165.

6. SBOp 4:383-492.

7. On Bernard's experience of his own misery, see *Aspects du monachisme hier et aujourd'hui* (Paris, 1968) 261-277; English translation, *Aspects of Monasticism* (Kalamazoo, 1978) 251-266.

8. On this chronology, see SBOp 4:119.

show himself to his monks, and to the general public, with such sincerity?

Again in the Prologue to the book on *Precept and Dispensation*, he seems to be what we might term (in keeping with a thematic existential) a problematic man: he is divided and makes no secret of it. He confesses that he has long hesitated to respond to repeated urgings 'forced' (*cogitis*) upon him either to show his incapacity or to lack charity. Finally, when he freely decided to accept, he leapt with courage, as it were, 'into an abyss from which one is not sure—God alone knows—whether one will emerge'.[9]   It is significant that, having been petitioned to write by two monks whose names he does not give, harshly. Consciousness of his own authority led him to respect the authority of other superiors, without respecting the problems of rank and file religious as we today would expect. But he proved a certain detachment from both the content and the style of what he proposed to write, and he included many expressions of modesty.

2. *Importance of intentions.* Did Bernard practice such careful analysis of his own and other people's motivations when he was in the thick of the fray? He seems to have been aware of the possible illusions waiting to trap him if he intervened for his own profit. We notice this in the precautions he took against such a danger. In his letters about the election at York, he constantly stressed that he was intervening in the interest of the Church and not his own. He could have been unaware that he possessed human reasons and a certain tendency to exert his influence. Even to our day, a reading from the Breviary of York reproaches the adversaries of William Fitzherbert with having been too eager for power.[10] But, on the other hand, is it not a proof of maturity that he

9. SBOp 3:253-254.
10. Quoted by Bruno Scott James, *St. Bernard of Clairvaux* (London, 1957) 151.

used all this inner energy in the service of a cause he believed to be just, as a sort of pedagogy intended to make
others—in the first place the popes—serve this same cause in
the only way he considered good? One of the ways Bernard
used to pressure people was to insist, not only on the cause
itself (in this case, the objective good of the Church of
York), but also on the difference between the motivations
of each candidates supporters. To Innocent II, he wrote in
Letter 347: 'Those who come on my behalf are seeking not
their interests, but those of Jesus Christ. Their only motivation is the love of God. I do not think that even their worst
enemies could suspect them of being inspired in this business either by their own interests or by personal resentment.
If then anyone is of God, let him stand by them'.[11] Such a
challenge hurled at the pope supposes that at least, for Bernard, intentions are important.

3. *The courage to act.* Having acknowledged his limits and
verified his motives, Bernard got down to deciding to act. If
we are to believe him, action cost him. In all his Prologues
he tells of the fear he felt each time he was going to under-
take a new work. Such fear can be paralysing, like the fear
that prevents a parachutist from jumping into space. If he
pays attention to the apprehension he cannot move; if he
overcomes it, he shows he can face danger. In the same way,
Bernard could start building up his person if he overcame
his hesitation to write or to act; his ego *in full expansion* allowed him to master the different fears he felt and had already admitted in the Prologue to *The Steps of Humility and
Pride.* From that time on, he took a very realistic view of
himself; his personality was sufficiently developed for him
to commit himself 'to the extent of his capabilities'.[12] But,
using words of Saint John already quoted in the Rule of

11. PL 182:552.
12. SBOp 3:16.

Saint Benedict, he declared what it was that gave him his strength: charity. He had to do more than just fulfill self; he had to outdo himself and go onto God.

He says so again in the Prologue to the homilies *In Praise of the Virgin Mother*:[13] we must make a virtue of necessity. The words *necesse est*, *necessitas* and *necessaria*, which he uses in the space of three lines, reveal the kinds of obligation which others imposed upon him and which, in this case, circumstances favored, for illness kept him living on the margin of his community and thus gave him leisure for writing. Yet he did not let himself be conditioned either by the requests he received or by circumstances: he kept his freedom—*dum tamen ex hoc non impediar*—also to satisfy his personal devotion.

This 'necessity' to which he consented is cited again in the Prologue of the *Apologia*[14] and in the letter which presented the treatise to William of Saint Thierry.[15] Bernard's very keen sense of authority is apparent at the beginning of almost all his works, when he says he has been ordered to write and that he has complied. Was this due to the education one received in a noble family, and in knightly circles where it was usual to command? That there was in him a tendency to dominate is certain: this only leads us to admire all the more his ability to obey, in order to serve, once he has understood that this is his duty. He says clearly to the abbot of Saint Thierry: 'Up to now, whenever you have ordered me to write a work, I have done so in spite of myself, or else I have utterly refused'.[16] In this way he claimed total independence, his right to refuse, and the use he sometimes made of it. The great wealth of his personality comes from this conciliation within himself of master and servant.

13. SBOp 4:13.
14. SBOp 3:81.
15. *Ibid.*, p. 15.
16. *Ibid.*

Any 'timidity' in him brought up first of all a defense mechanism, a reaction, and may sometimes even have made him aggressive in affirming his autonomy. Then he considered his two possibilities: in the case of the urgent cause which William of Saint Thierry claimed it is his duty to serve, he did not shy away from his responsibilities. He gave Cistercians and Cluniacs the dressing-down he was asked to deliver. This opened him to a new danger of which he was very conscious and which he clearly denounced, not without some slight exaggeration, which is one of the forms of humor. This new danger lay in setting himself up as 'judge of the whole world.' This tendency also had to be purified and mastered, and this presupposes that it is recognized. From his viewpoint then, in moments when he calmly decided to intervene, it was not easy to act; for he had to control all those reasons which would incline him to do so. In such cases Bernard appears as his own master; he succeeded in dominating his spontaneous drives, and made his intentions consistent with his actions.

4. *Freedom of speech.* The way which Bernard had of being sincere with himself gave him the right to be so with others. In the paragraph of the *Apologia* which follows the introduction and where he questioned himself in the manner we have just seen, there, he indulged in abuse against hypocrisy. The word 'Woe!' (*Vae*), inspired by the curses in the Gospels and the Apocalypse, recurs five times here in formulas, the last of which is: 'Woe, I say, and again woe!'.[17] This forceful language of studied and willed violence is well in keeping with his way of acting.

His care to be frank and clear resulted not only from literary requirements: it was a psychological need, and could become a means of 'building up charity', as Bernard expressed the wish to do in the Prologue to his treatise *On*

---

17. *Apologia*, 2:SBOp 3:82.

Grace and Free Choice: there, in connection with an 'obscure' subject, he wanted to attempt to carry out the precept of Scripture which says 'They who explain me shall have life everlasting'.[18] This clarity of style was his style of life.

And Bernard always spoke his mind whenever he had to. In the Prologue to Letter 42 *On the Duty and Function of Bishops*, addressing one of the greatest prelates of France, the archbishop of Sens, who had asked him to write, he refused to be accommodating.[19] Throughout his text he unambiguously denounced what he thought it is his duty to reproach in the church dignitaries of his times. Fighting this way against all mediocrity, he ran the serious risk of making enemies among the higher clergy, even though he had need of them, if only on behalf of the abbeys he founded. But he courageously exposes himself to this eventuality. Moreover, he quoted a lot of Scripture, as he had already done at the beginning of the *Apologia*.

Was this a means for Bernard to hide himself behind an authority which could defend him? Or did it allow him to give free rein, under cover of holy words, to his own aggressiveness? Or again, did he realize that his own thoughts might appear to him to be the truth, a message that was too personal and that he wanted to make universal by expressing it, or confirming it, through God's spokesmen? These various possibilities are probably all at work in his writings: it is necessary to determine the reality in each case. But at least we cannot help admiring the great wealth of the words of God he used. More than once, his own drives were, so to speak, sifted through the sieve of sacred language. In many places he says that we have to experience what we read in Scripture: that is what he did. He deeply interiorized numerous verses of the Bible, lived them with great intensity, and

18. *Ibid.*, p. 165, citing Si 24:31.
19. PL 182:803.

made them his own. This entailed the danger, mentioned above in connection with self-assertion, of identifying the Word of God and his own aspirations, instead of bringing these into line with the intentions of the inspired authors. Nothing is ever absolutely pure when a man says something in God's name. But, certainly, one of the sources of Bernard's spiritual energy came to him from the conviction that he could rest on an authority greater than himself.

II. VALUES, NORMS OF ACTION

This last consideration leads us to notice something that sheds light on all Bernard's conduct and partly explains it: he was conscious of having a message to proclaim; he was convinced he was to serve higher realities. These may be described as values, in the sense which many philosophers, especially psychologists, have given this word in speaking of objective facts considered preferable to subjective views.

1. *The search for meaning.* Let us point out to start with that Bernard had a surprising aptitude for interpreting the events and circumstances which marked his life in a religious, even a sacred perspective. This is seen as early as the Prologue of his homilies *In Praise of the Virgin Mother*, if— as seems likely— what William of Saint Thierry says firmly in Book One of the *First Life*, about the special love Aleth, Bernard's mother, had for her son and the affection he kept for her after her death when he was fourteen or fifteen years old. At the beginning of his abbacy, he was obliged by sickness to take care of himself and to take a rest away from common life. This gave him 'some leisure'. It pleased him then to 'satisfy his own devotion' and give in to a drive he had often felt to write something about the Virgin

Mother.[20] Quite naturally, from a psychological point of view, we wonder whether this strong, independent temperament did not feel a need for affective dependency, like that of a son for his mother when they had had a relationship of the kind William of Saint Thierry describes. Aleth had wanted him to know that total gift of self to God which led him to the solitude of Cîteaux. And now he was temporarily separated from his community and alone with God. It is understandable that he should have considered his situation a spiritual experience, one to which he was keen to give meaning by relating it to the Mother of God.

We find the same insistence on 'devotion' and 'zeal for prayer' in his letter to William of Saint Thierry, who had asked him to write the *Apologia*.[21] But there, as in the first page of this treatise, we find the necessity he felt to interpret events, his friend's requests, and to see in them so many signs manifesting a will of God to which he could not refuse to submit.[22]

In the two Prologues we have just quoted, Bernard affirmed the priority he gave, in his opinion, to prayer. At the beginning of the homilies on the Virgin Mother, he set down another of his criteria for decision, one always presupposed elsewhere, namely, the 'service of his brothers'.[23] Likewise, in the Prologue to Letter 77, in the form of a *Treatise on Baptism* responding to questions put to him by Hugh of Saint Victor, Bernard expressly said that he wanted to act as a 'servant of God'.[24] If he agreed to write, he did so not simply to please a friend, who was also a respected teacher, but because the desire to serve was deeply rooted in him.

2. *The need for surpassing the self.* The first of the values

---

20. SBOp 4:13.
21. SBOp 3:64.
22. *Ibid.*, p. 82.
23. *Ibid.*, p. 13.
24. SBOp 7:184, 16-17.

Bernard served was the love of God, expressed in prayers and not the object of speculative knowledge, but a lived reality, an experience. To write about it was the 'sweetest, the surest, and the most useful thing' that could be done, as three absolute comparatives have it in the Prologue to the treatise *On the Love of God*.[25] Bernard set this love above everything else, but he also saw in it the means for the ego to attain total self-fulfillment, to fulfill self in surpassing self. And this could not be the result of his effort alone: grace was necessary, and he had to ask for it. In the second draft of sermon twenty-four on the Song—which is really a prologue written after the long interruption of his stay in Rome during the schism— Bernard repeated that he was 'obliged' to others, that he 'lived by their merits', that he could not continue writing unless 'God, answering his faithful plea, grants he may give what he does not possess'.[26] And often, in the course of this great work, he asks that we pray for him that he may bring it to a good end. This was in keeping with patristic tradition; but it seem more than a literary theme here: Bernard's conviction that he could only become completely himself by concerning himself with something beyond him.

Here again he was keen to integrate into the oneness of his life of union with God and, of his contemplative thought, the church experiences which he had just had. And we suspect too that the need he seems to have had to speak continually of his limited capacity for writing was not just artifice. In humiliating himself, in professing modesty, he set up in himself some consistency between his timidity and his need to dominate, between his life of intense activity and his longing for contemplation. By this form of ascesis which heals a sort of tension, even an inner contradiction, he constantly made up his own personal synthesis. He could not

25. SBOp 3:119.
26. SBOp 1:151.

live continuously in competition with others; he needed
unity. He sought and found it in God.

3. *Towards the maturity of adulthood.* This unity acquired
by surpassing self was already the major theme of the first
of the *Sermons on the Song of Songs* , where Bernard explains that 'human wisdom' is not enough to give meaning
to the existence of those who are occupied with God and
spend their life 'meditating his law'.[27] This man, whose
style reveals straightaway that he is an artist, a man with a
passion for beauty, had the courage to set in the background
both letters and intellectual knowledge of God. The whole of
this introductory sermon becomes a song exulting in the
marvels of God and arises, with an unfeignable conviction,
from gratitude, joy, and the hope of a personality entirely
open to the highest values. What he aspired to was an 'experience'. He wanted to teach those of his readers who had
already attained adulthood how to leap, as it were, from
what they knew to what they lived. Did he live out this program himself? At least he understood that it was important
and he excelled at teaching it. And in this connection he
formulated perfectly the law of psychology which says that
the ripe age which follows the infant stage of 'the childish
soul' is not attained simply by the passage of time, but is
acquired at the cost of an inner experience 'made up of efforts and merits'.[28]

In the course of this first sermon, Bernard had already
pointed out one of the fruits of this maturity: it alone allows
us to begin without danger the reading and the commentary
of this 'song of the bed-chamber', this 'nuptial song' which
is the Song of songs. It is maturity which makes possible the
sublimation allowing, throughout the work, to speak without
either shame or guilt of the joys of human love and to rise,

27. *Ibid.*, pp. 3-8.
28. *Ibid.*, p. 8.

form them, to the contemplation of the mystery of charity.

Another indication of his maturity is the liberty he retained about what people thought of him, whether good or
bad. In the first case—as in his Letter 87, to canon Oger,—he
brought the praises heaped on him down to their proper
proportions.[29] In the second, it was enough for him to know
he had acted in accord with his conscience to accept the
criticism aimed at him without being discouraged. This is
what he did at the beginning of the second book *On Consideration* in regard to those who accused him of having
caused the failure of the second crusade.[30] Sometimes he
foresaw the reproaches and accepted what was coming, as in
the Prologue to *In Praise of a New Knighthood*: 'If someone
is not satisfied with this, or if it seems inadequate to them, I
shall be nonetheless content, since I have not failed to give
you my best.'[31] Bernard's concern was with being at the disposal of his friend and relative Hugh of Payns, master of the
Templars. His reputation as a writer came second. In the
same way, in the first sermon on the Song, he says he was
giving in to the request of a friend whom we know to be the
Carthusian, Bernard of Portes.[32] And at the beginning of the
second draft of sermon twenty-four, after the interruption
caused by his third journey to Rome, he again protested that
he was incapable of writing about something sublime after
having been absorbed by other, very inferior worries.[33]
There is in all this probably some imagined modesty, a literary theme. But there is nothing to prevent us from seeing
there some sincerity, too, for one of the marks of maturity is
to acknowledge one's limitations and to set more value by
an upright will than by competency.

---

29. See above, ch. IV, pp. 95-98.
30. SBOp 3:410-443.
31. *Ibid.*, p. 213; CF 19:128.
32. Cp. *Recueil d'études* 1:194-196.
33. SBOp 1:151.

III. THE INTEGRATION OF NEEDS TO VALUES

1. *Early yet unending progress.* The suggestions which have just been put forward lead us perhaps to a right concept of what holiness meant to Bernard of Clairvaux. It is not a matter of knowing whether or not it was right to canonize him. In all Churches, as long as canonization has been practised, the official declaration of holiness corresponds partly to sociological and sometimes political norms by which the role played by christian men and women is measured, and not only to the fact that their virtues are supposed to have been flawless.[34] Evdokimov, for example, has written: 'In former times, the holy princes were canonized, not in virtue of their personal holiness, but for their faithfulness to the charisms of royal power used in the service of the christian people'.[35] In the case of Bernard, even his contemporaries, given the role he had played before their eyes, considered that he had behaved in keeping with his charisms, which were exceptional, as a monk, abbot, and man of the Church. Furthermore, all his teaching, oral and written, gave a program of holiness to the people of his day and to posterity: and in this perspective there is absolutely no doubt that he should have been canonized.

But how did he live out this program, how did he bring his private virtue and his public role into harmony? This is the question that must be asked, at the end of a search for truth which has attempted to discern the saint he really was, beyond the image others have given him, beyond the image drawn out of his teaching. A certain psychological analysis can contribute to this by discerning, beyond the ideas he ex-

---

34. Cp. P. Delooz, *Sociologie et canonisation* (The Hague, 1969). Other works by the same author are quoted in 'Deux nouveaux Docteurs de l'Église', in *La vie spirituelle* 123 (1970) 136-138.

35. P. Evdokimov, *L'amour fou de Dieu* (Paris, 1973) 134.

pressed, what drove and deeply motivated him. It does seem that at all periods of his life, human passions coexisted in him with a sublime ideal. It would be easy, and reassuring, from an apologetic point of view, to be able to declare that we see in him an evolution in the course of which he never ceased to purify himself, and consequently to progress, in keeping with a formula which he himself gave and which D. Knowles applied to him: 'No one remains the same in virtue or in love; not to go forward is to go back.'[36] The same historian added; 'St Bernard in 1150 is not the Bernard of 1120; in the young abbot we may detect excess, exaggeration, violence, rhetoric; in the mature saint we should use great circumspection in our judgement.'[37]

In reality, as early as his first works he offered both signs of a temperament given to extremes, and evidence of balance in his ideas. And the same is true in the works of his final years, as *On Consideration*. He himself taught, as we have seen, that maturity comes more from inner experience than from the accumulation of years. It is the fruit of a constant struggle which may begin early and is never finished. All his life he was a fighting man, acquainted with failure and success, sorrows and joys. In his adolescent years, he mourned his mother; as a young man, he managed to convert his kinsmen to the cistercian observance; as a young abbot he was disappointed to see his cousin Robert prefer Cluny to Cîteaux and Arnold of Morimond unfaithful to what he considered to be the only legitimate way of being faithful to a vocation. Perhaps in his last years suffering became harder, with the treason of his favorite secretary, Nicolas of Montièraney, the failure of the second crusade, his disagreement with his former disciple, Eugene III, and finally the death of several of his close relatives and friends. But the sadnesses

36. David Knowles, *The Historian and Character and Other Essays* (Cambridge, 1963) p. 7.
37. *Ibid.*, p. 8.

did not prevent him from maintaining the ardent joy which is expressed, for example, in the last *Sermons on the Song*.

Only a painstaking examination of all his texts or books written about him, taken in chronological order, to the extent that this is known, would allow us to say whether, and in what direction, we discern an evolution in the way he reconciled his temperament with his ideal. Meanwhile, until this vast analysis is undertaken, it was legitimate here to follow only an approximate chronology—as we did the first part of the chapter—and to turn our research to certain behavior, symbolic of his entire conduct, which is then examined from different points of view and in different areas. Thus it has been possible to suggests some progression, ideal or logical, from a declaring of inner conflicts to outstripping them by serving supra-individual values. The important thing has been that each observation or interpretation has been founded on specific texts. Now, after having, as it were, pulled apart this assembly of psychological, literary, and spiritual data which constitutes Bernard's own evidence in himself, the time has now come to try and rebuild his personality.

2. *Needs and motivations.* If we want to try and see how Bernard's personality was organized, it seems we may distinguish three levels. On the level Bernard wanted to dominate, which in this sense we may describe as the superior one, we find the values he consciously professed: esteem for the cistercian way of life, zeal for the Church and commitment to its service, charity inspiring the desire to give everyone the spiritual advice necessary to each, the love of God, and the need to pray. These motivations and others of the same kind were inspired directly by Gospel principles we often hear quoted: the thirst for justice and the will to do good to others. This is the spiritual level, the one where, in the long run, we reach holiness.

On the level of psychology, which in itself has nothing to

do with holiness, we discern in Bernard a number of natural needs, temperamental drives which can be reduced to a tendency to aggression and a propensity to dominate.

On the level between these two, come into play those defense mechanisms by which Bernard attempted to justify his needs by bringing them into line with his motivations. This is where he rationalized his tendencies, and tried to justify the manifestation of them and, consequently, it is the area of the ascesis of intentions. This takes lucidity and courage; the first is a matter of humility, and the second a question of detachment from self: we have to surpass ourselves in order to run the risk of acting in conformity with the principles we profess.

If the spiritual level is where we reach holiness, if the psychological level provides the matter for getting there, then the level of reasoned and willed justification is where grace and human effort marry with a view to domination, mastering, purifying, and unifying natural, anarchic, and unconscious tendencies. But it is also the level where the illusion can creep in of legitimating temperamental needs by principles taken as objective. We may say that this is the level where we really fight for holiness. It is as if we have to pass from aggressiveness to passion, or, to put it more exactly, from human passions to a great passion for God and his work in the world, a passion which in its turn will comprehend and utilize all the psychic dynamisms of a man of flesh and blood, integrating them into his elected ideal. For aggressiveness is in itself neither good nor bad: it is neutral and part of the human nature of every normal person.[38] Its value depends on the use we make of it and the meaning we give it by orienting it towards an end which transcends it. It must become a means in the service of love.

---

38. This has often been stressed by psychologists, for example, Barry McLaughlin, *Nature, Grace and Religious Development* (Westminster, Md., 1964) 95-98.

3. *A man of God who remains a man*. Did Bernard accomplish this integration? We can answer neither yes nor no; the reply has to be qualified. After an objective examination, as impartial as possible, of much of his behavior—while waiting for all of it to be examined—, it seems we may say that Bernard did achieve integration, but with the two following reservations: first, it was not natural to him but required his constant effort; secondly, he never totally achieved it. But it was none the less a success, for in this there is no total and absolute success: success lies in the effort itself and it even supposes the awareness and acceptance of failure. We find all that in Bernard.

He was well aware of not being perfect: not only did he know it, but he said so and wrote it because he wanted it to be known. And we realize how necessary this admission was: even in our own day, his works are admired, and it would be surprising if he were not aware of his talent. And had this been the case, he would have learned about it from the praise his contemporaries insisted on giving his style and his thought.[39] Furthermore, he could not have helped noticing he was esteemed and, something to which every person is more sensitive, loved. Much evidence in this sense has already been collected. It is easy to explain why he was held in such affection: in most cases he showed himself encouraging, full of kindness, pleasantness, and joy.[40] He was

---

39. *Études sur S. Bernard, Analecta SOC* 9:1-2 (Rome, 1953) 123-124, and *Recueil d'études sur S. Bernard* II:350-351.

40. To the evidence cited in this sense in 'S. Bernard et la dévotion joyeuse', in *S. Bernard homme d' Église* (Paris, 1953) pp. 238-240, we may add the following: William of Saint Thierry, *Vita prima S. Bernardi* 1.33 (*PL* 185:246): 'modo illo suo generoso arridens nobis'. Clarembald of Arras: 'jucundae recordationis abbas Bernardus', cited by H. Vaupel,'Clarembaldus von Arras und Walter von Mortagne' in '*Zeitschrift für Kirchensgescichte*' 65 (1953-1954) 134; Geoffrey of Auxerre, *Super Apocalypsim* 7, ed. F. Gastaldelli (Rome, 1970) pp. 115,116: 'Quam dulcissime nobis pater noster Bernardus dum adviveret...'; Godescalc, abbot of the Premonstratensians of Seelan, in the diocese of Prague, who in a letter of 1184, made known to the Chapter of

appreciated, not by all, but by many people, in very different circles. And we have the proof that he was able to distance himself from the judgement men made of him.[41]

Several years before his death, he was already considered a saint, and someone decided to write his life without telling him, *nec ipso sciente*. Had he known, what would he have thought? In other words, did Bernard of Clairvaux know he was Saint Bernard? He could not help knowing he was a great writer, a great abbot, a great churchman. But did he also think he was great in the order of sanctity? Surely not, if this supposes the absence of temptations and faults: he spoke publicly about both, in connection with himself.[42] Likely he would have approved the analysis made of him by a group of psychologists who had worked with his texts. I asked one of them who, thinking particularly about his reaction to the Song of Songs, said ' He is a hundred percent man'. 'Is he also a saint?', I asked. And the group as a whole answered, 'yes'. 'But is he a hundred percent saint'? I insisted. And the first speaker retorted without hesitating: 'He wanted to be a hundred percent'. Now, is this not what counts in the eyes of God and those who try to judge as He does? To what extent did Bernard achieve what he willed? That is God's secret. As for Bernard himself, the proof of his holiness probably is to be found in the fact that he never claimed to have got there.

If Bernard was sometimes ironical, even sarcastic, about other people, he often poked fun at himself. Historians ought

---

Cîteaux a vision he had: *'Cum ecce subito flos et gemma ordinis vestri, sanctus Bernardus, quem nunquam in carne videram, hilariter apparuit et instrumenta duorum baculorum, quos cruccas vocant, ostendit, quibus suffultus, eum intra iucundissimum palatium secutus sum...'*.

41. See Letter 87 and the article cited above section III, n.10.

42. On these temptations, see *Aspects du monachisme*. In Letter 70 Bernard confessed to having had a violent angry reaction; see *Études sur S. Bernard*, pp. 190-191, and *Recueil d'études sur S. Bernard* 2I: pp. 319-326.

to keep this same attitude in their judgements. Noticing his skill in political manoeuvres and the literary talent he used to advance it, they have a tendency to be harsh with him, and to distrust the motivations he said were pure: were they really? Was he as detached, as free in his mind, as he said he was? God alone knows. He certainly spoke very well about purity of intention; he excelled in recommending it to others. He has a full blown teaching on the subject. But to what extent did he practice it? Was there always consistency between his spiritual teaching, his psychological attitudes, his political conduct and, lastly, his ideas? We hardly dare say that this was always the case.

But did this partial failure prevent him from being both a sinner and a justified man? In some cases he enjoyed giving vent to his anger and his zeal for the interests of the Lord and the Church, and that was for him a way of strengthening himself in the conviction that he was serving a just cause. Except in the case where he repented afterwards—as with his brother Bartholomew, according to Letter 70—, he gives the impression that his outbursts were controlled, and even willed: they were means for attaining his end. Perhaps, when it came to fights he was a little unscrupulous in the means he used. Is it enough, in order to be a saint, to have upright intentions, ordered to charity? Is it possible to have a clean heart and dirty hands at the same time? More than one historian thinks that Bernard's hands were not always clean, and, had he known all that historians know, he would probably have agreed. He would have admitted that he was not always sufficiently well informed about facts, circumstances, teachings, and people. But is the saint necessarily a perfectly balanced being and a Christian who commits no sin, even supposing that such a person ever existed except in the only instance which God took human nature? We dare not here appeal to the mystery of Jesus' angry outbursts—and, he alone, was totally holy.

And if, for example, Bernard was excessive in identifying

God's will with his own, were there not excuses? Had he not been superior for a long time, in a day when the exercise of authority entailed this danger more than at other periods? His authoritarianism must not lead us to forget his spirit of service, nor his aggressiveness the many instances when he made peace. And, on the whole, ought we not in reading his texts set them in historical context made up of a certain intolerance and, as we would say today, integrism? In those days, holiness consisted in doing great things, and Bernard did them. For example, did his efforts as a founder of monasteries not arise from a need for achievement, and from his personal charm rather than from his aggressiveness and his tendency to dominate, to exert influence? We can only venture to ask questions of this kind, and the answers will elude us as they eluded him. For here we are on the misty frontier which at once unites yet separates a human personality and holiness, the gift of the Holy Spirit. Bernard had a strong personality, and we may even say a healthy personality. He gives every sign of this: self-confidence, autonomy, and freedom over against his milieu, an ability for taking decisions and initiative, a consciousness of his limitations, a perception of the world's needs, a faculty for involving himself in very diverse causes, all of them lofty. On the balance, honestly, there is more light than shadow.

And yet between psychic good health and holiness there is a no-man's-land which remains obscure to the human eye, a distance which remains uncrossed and which prevents even the healthiest of personalities from coinciding with a totally holy christian life. Saint Bernard teaches us that it is possible to be a man of God without ceasing to be a man. A saint may be a man, or a woman, who is normally without vice, but not without faults—for we must not be afraid to admit it—nor without sins. The saint is a Christian who remains a sinner, in the unique way proper to each person's gifts and limits, the form of humility granted him at the cost of humiliations which are his own secret. If Bernard was humble in this way, everything is all right from the point of view of his relationship with God. The same God who made him aggressive also made him humble, not without Bernard himself doing his best to be less aggressive and more humble. Who dares to pass judgement on this mystery?

Tradition teaches that holiness supposes unity but does not do away with contrasts, and that it culminates in humility, not in grandeur. A syrian monk of the seventh century, Isaac of Nineveh, wrote: 'The person who knows his sins is greater than the one who raises a dead man to life.... Someone who knows his own weakness is greater than someone who sees the angels. The person who, solitary and sorrowful, follows Christ, is greater than the person who enjoys the favor of crowds in the churches...'.[43] Bernard had known acclaim by the crowds and often approval by the great. But where he showed himself to be a saint was in the knowledge of his shortcomings, the admission of his failings, and in spite of these his faithfulness in following Christ.

43. Isaac of Nineveh, *Discourse* 34.

CISTERCIAN PUBLICATIONS INC.

Kalamazoo, Michigan

TITLES LISTING

THE CISTERCIAN FATHERS SERIES

THE WORKS OF
BERNARD OF CLAIRVAUX

Texts and Studies
in the
Monastic Tradition

THE WORKS OF WILLIAM OF
SAINT THIERRY

THE WORKS OF
AELRED OF RIEVAULX

THE WORKS OF GILBERT OF
HOYLAND

THE WORKS OF JOHN OF FORD

OTHER EARLY CISTERCIAN WRITERS

* *Temporarily out of print*   † *Forthcoming*

THE CISTERCIAN STUDIES SERIES

MONASTIC TEXTS

CHRISTIAN SPIRITUALITY

MONASTIC STUDIES

CISTERCIAN STUDIES

Saint Gregory Nazianzen: Selected Poems

Eight Chapters on Perfection and Angel's Song
(Walter Hilton)

Creative Suffering (Iulia de Beausobre)

Bringing Forth Christ. Five Feasts of the Child
Jesus (St Bonaventure)

Gentleness in St John of the Cross

Distributed in North America only for Fairacres Press.

DISTRIBUTED BOOKS

St Benedict: Man with An Idea (Melbourne Studies)

The Spirit of Simplicity

Benedict's Disciples (David Hugh Farmer)

The Emperor's Monk: A Contemporary Life of
Benedict of Aniane

A Guide to Cistercian Scholarship (2nd ed.)

*North American customers may order
through booksellers or directly from
the publisher:*

    Cistercian Publications
    St Joseph's Abbey
    Spencer, Massachusetts 01562
    (508) 885-7011

    Cistercian Publications
    Editorial Offices
    WMU Station
    Kalamazoo, Michigan 49008
    (616) 387-5090

*A complete catalogue of texts-in-
translation and studies on early,
medieval, and modern Christian
monasticism is available at no
cost from Cistercian Publications.*

*Cistercian monks and nuns have been
living lives of prayer & praise, meditation
& manual labor since the twelfth century.
They are part of an unbroken tradition
which extends back to the fourth century
and which continues today in the Catholic
church, the Orthodox churches, the
Anglican communion, and most recently,
in the Protestant churches.*

*Share their way of life and their search for
God by reading Cistercian Publications.*